How To Buy Bonds
The Smart Way

☆ ☆ ☆ ☆ ☆

Investment Books by Stephen Littauer

Grow Rich with Mutual Funds—Without a Broker

How To Build a Fortune—Investing in Your Spare Time

How To Buy Bonds the Smart Way

How To Buy Mutual Funds the Smart Way

How To Buy Stocks the Smart Way

How To Buy Bonds
The Smart Way

☆ ☆ ☆ ☆ ☆

Stephen Littauer

Dearborn
Financial Publishing, Inc.

This publication is designed to provide accurate and authoritative information in regard to the subject matter covered. It is sold with the understanding that the publisher is not engaged in rendering legal, accounting or other professional service. If legal advice or other expert assistance is required, the services of a competent professional person should be sought.

Managing Editor: Jack Kiburz
Senior Associate Editor: Karen A. Christensen
Interior Design: Lucy Jenkins
Cover Design: S. Laird Jenkins Corporation

Published by Dearborn Financial Publishing, Inc.®

Printed in the United States of America

96 97 98 10 9 8 7 6 5 4 3 2 1

Library of Congress Cataloging-in-Publication Data

Littauer, Stephen L.
    How to buy bonds the smart way / Stephen Littauer.
      p. cm.
    Includes index.
    ISBN 0-7931-1528-0 (pbk.)
    1. Bonds. I. Title.
HG4651.L569   1996
332.63'23—dc20
                                            95-4961
                                                CIP

Contents

☆ ☆ ☆ ☆ ☆ ☆ ☆ ☆ ☆ ☆ ☆ ☆ ☆ ☆ ☆ ☆ ☆ ☆

Preface

☆ ☆ ☆ ☆ ☆ ☆ ☆ ☆ ☆ ☆ ☆ ☆ ☆ ☆ ☆ ☆

Welcome to the profitable world of bonds! The bond market is huge. The U.S. Government is the world's largest borrower, with more than $3 trillion of U.S. Treasury securities outstanding. The mortgage-backed securities market totals more than $4 trillion, the corporate bond market is well over $2 trillion, and there are more than $1.4 trillion of municipal securities outstanding.

Like most investors today, you probably have some experience with fixed-income investments. You may have purchased certificates of deposit (CDs) at your local bank or savings institution. Perhaps you either gave or received U.S. savings bonds as gifts. Yet you can discover a vast array of income-generating alternatives in your search for yield and safety. No matter what your investment goals are today, you can find the fixed-income securities appropriate for your investment portfolio.

If you share such investment aims as building your portfolio, lowering your taxes, or building a steady retirement income, fixed-income securities can be right for you. This book is designed to give you the information you need to compare the different types of fixed-income securities and decide which may be most suitable for your investment goals. You'll probably find some new terms, so to make your reading easier I've also included a glossary.

Divided into three parts, *How To Buy Bonds the Smart Way* will give you the tools you need to invest successfully in fixed-income securities. Part I, "The Basics of Fixed-Income Securities," gives you the essentials on bonds: what they are and why they may be the best way for you to achieve a regular stream of income while protecting your assets. You will find out:

- which bonds are the safest of all investments and discover a $3 trillion market;
- which bonds will give you higher yields;

- where are the hidden, profitable opportunities that investors often overlook;
- what bonds pay federally tax-exempt interest; and
- how zero-coupon bonds grow in value.

A separate chapter explains how bonds are rated for safety. Our goal is to give you a firm grounding in the important aspects of fixed-income investing.

Part II, "Buying Bonds the Smart Way," shows you how to develop your own financial plan, and how fixed-income securities can provide for your most important investment objectives: safety, regular income, potential growth and minimization of income taxes. At the same time, you will understand how important is the relationship between risk and reward in your fixed-income investing. You will learn techniques experienced investors use to maximize their returns and find out why total return is more important than current yield alone. You'll find out how easily you can buy U.S. Treasury securities directly from the Federal Reserve, without paying any bank or broker fees.

Finally, you'll learn why *mutual funds* are a smart way to buy bonds - and how you can buy them without paying any sales charges or commissions. You'll also find important information on *fund shopping networks,* one of the newest services available to mutual fund buyers. Through these one-stop sources, you can purchase any of a wide range of funds without paying any sales charges to banks or investment brokers.

Part III, "The World of Bond Funds," introduces you to the major types of fixed-income mutual funds, each with its own unique characteristics. In each category, a specific fund is recommended that has produced superior results for its shareholders. If you are interested in a fund offering utmost safety of the securities in its portfolio, you can choose a fund that holds only U.S. Treasury or government-backed bonds. For higher current income (and greater risk) there are corporate bonds. Still higher income may be obtained from funds that invest in high-yield, but lower-rated securities.

For greatest diversification, you'll find valuable information about bond index funds, which seek to replicate the whole bond market (or important segments of it), and can help smooth out the income and value fluctuations common to all securities markets. To take advantage of the higher yields and total return potential sometimes available from debt securities abroad, you might consider international bond funds. If you are seeking both current income and capital growth, I'll show you bond funds with an equity "kicker." Some of these funds hold portfolios with both stocks and bonds. Other such funds own bonds that are convertible into common stock. Income and growth oriented funds are concerned with achieving the greatest total return (yield and growth of capital) for their shareholders.

If you are tax-weary, take a look at good tax-free municipal bond funds. The income dividends from these funds are generally exempt from federal income taxes. Even triple-tax-free funds exist, exempt from federal, state and local taxes.

Finally, if you are one of those people who like a bargain, you'll find the section on closed-end bond funds a treasure hunt for good deals. These funds are traded on major securities exchanges and often can be bought at a price lower than their net asset value.

This book appeals to investors of all ages. Fixed-income securities may be right for you if you are concerned with building a portfolio, achieving a steady retirement income, or lowering your taxes. Whether your goals are short- or long-term, you can find many potentially rewarding fixed-income investments, each with its unique set of characteristics.

So get your bond'$ worth out of your investments!

1

Investing
in Bonds

Bonds are actually loans or IOUs, an acknowledgement by the issuer that money has been borrowed and is to be repaid to the bondholder at a specified rate of interest over a predetermined period of time. These instruments are referred to as *debt obligations,* contrasted with stocks, which represent ownership of a corporation, usually with the right to vote and receive dividends.

As with most loans, issuers of bonds pay interest for the temporary use of money. The amount borrowed is the principal, or face value, of the bond. The interest you receive is called the bond yield and is expressed as a percentage of the bond's face value. For example, if you pay $1,000 for a bond that pays interest of $80 per year, the bond is said to yield 8 percent ($80/$1,000). Since your income from the bond generally doesn't vary from year to year, bonds are called *fixed-income securities.*

Fixed-income securities form the centerpiece of most individual investors' portfolios and with good reason, too. Bonds have lower but steadier returns than stocks, and represent the most reliable source of income. In addition, when added to a portfolio of stocks, bonds act as a stabilizer because they reduce the volatility of your overall returns. And while bonds will also reduce the growth potential of your portfolio below that of stocks alone, the real advantage of stock/bond diversification is that it lowers your risk more than it lowers your potential return.

A successful long-term financial plan depends to a large degree on how you allocate your assets, striking the right balance between bonds, stocks and cash reserves. See Chapter 9, *Start with a Financial Plan,* for help in setting your investment objectives.

Avoiding Mistakes Through Active Management

Bonds are traded on national securities exchanges and, like stocks, often sell for more or less than their intrinsic value. This occurs mainly because investors overreact to transitory events in the market-place or have difficulty understanding today's complex instruments. The best fixed-income investment managers use systematic analytical techniques to identify the best values in the market—bonds yielding more than appropriate for the risks they entail—and construct optimal bond portfolios.

Many investors mistakenly believe that the best way to invest in bonds is to buy them at issuance and hold them until maturity. But this approach ignores meaningful opportunities to avoid risk and add return. People often focus on yield, believing that higher yields will lead to higher returns. But in reality, yield is a poor indication of total return, which includes capital gains and/or losses in addition to interest earned and determines how the market value of your portfolio has grown. In contrast, managers of many of the best-performing bond mutual funds seek to maximize total returns through active management. They continuously monitor the bond markets in search of sectors, securities and maturity combinations that hold the greatest return potential.

While the interest paid on issued bonds generally remain fixed, general interest rates, credit ratings, yield curves and market conditions are constantly changing. Buying a portfolio of bonds and putting them aside with the intention of holding them until maturity, means you'll miss attractive investment opportunities as they come along and leave yourself vulnerable to new and unanticipated risks. And even if you're willing to forgo opportunity and take on risk for the sake of predictable interest income, you can't be sure about your own future needs. With a buy-and-hold strategy, you may end up locking yourself into a bond that you will later need to liquidate at a low point in its market value. Generally, active management of a bond portfolio is far more profitable and prudent than buy-and-hold investing.

Managing Risk in Bond Portfolios

Many top managers of fixed-income investment portfolios like to maintain the duration, or interest-rate sensitivity, of their portfolios at levels close to those of short-term bonds (those with maturities of 1 to 5 years) and intermediate-term bonds (those with maturities of 5 to 10 years). Duration is a risk-measuring gauge that provides a means of measuring in advance how much a bond or bond investment will rise or fall in value when interest rates change. It takes into account not only the maturity of an interest-bearing investment, but also the present and future flow of interest payments. This produces a figure, stated in years, that can be multiplied by a percentage-point change in interest rates to get the percentage change you can expect in the price of an investment. The rule of thumb: The longer the maturity, the greater the price change in response to interest-rate changes.

Shorter duration gives portfolios the risk/reward characteristics of short and intermediate bonds. Short-term bonds generally outperform money market investments with little more volatility, while intermediates are much safer than long-term bonds yet offer about the same income and return.

The investor who is searching for the right combination of yield and safety faces many investment choices. Banks offer federally insured money market accounts and certificates of deposits. But bank rates generally have not been competitive in recent years as the banking industry works to boost its profitability.

The yield can pick up substantially when moving from bank deposits to a variety of short- and long-term debt instruments. Money market funds offer "money market" rates and an expectation of principal stability, though without the protection of federal deposit insurance. And, because interest rates on long-term instruments are significantly higher today, the yield of longer-term bonds can be well above that of money market funds. The risk of progressively larger fluctuations in principal value is the tradeoff an investor must accept for higher yields and more durable income. Listed on the next page are the average yields of various categories of debt instruments in early 1995.

Categories	*Average Yields*
Tax-free money market funds	3.85%
Taxable money market funds	5.25
U.S. Treasury bills (13-week)	5.72
U.S. Treasury notes (5-year)	7.82
U.S. Treasury bonds (30-year)	7.87
High-grade corporate bonds	8.34
Intermediate-grade cporate bonds	8.97
Tax-free municipal bonds	6.92

However, the age-old warning of "caveat emptor" definitely applies. Selecting investments on the basis of yield alone can be dangerous to your wealth. Higher yield is usually associated with higher risks. Higher risks generally arise from lower credit quality or longer maturities. Lower credit quality involves the risk of default, that is, the failure of an issuer to make principal or interest payments when due.

How the Yield Curve Works

After you have decided on your investment objectives, and what kind of an investor you are, your challenge is to find a comfortable balance between risk and reward. In the world of fixed-income investments, a useful tool in attaining that balance is the "yield curve," a graph that correlates bond yields to maturities. Using the curve's rate structure as a reference, you can assemble a bond portfolio that correlates with your investment objectives and tolerance for risk. For example, Figure 1.1 illustrates the Treasury yield curve on April 19, 1995, showing the percentage yields of selected Treasury securities.

As a bond buyer, you need to be aware of the fundamental relationship between a bond's yield (its interest income) and its maturity. Longer maturities generally, but not always, translate into higher coupon rates (a bond's stated interest rate) because of the increased potential that, over time, a rise in interest rates will lower bond prices.

Generally, bond values move in the opposite direction from interest rates. Thus, if interest rates go up, the price of bonds will decline. Conversely, when interest rates go down, the value of bonds will rise. For example, suppose you own a $1,000 face amount bond that pays 8 percent ($80 per year) and want to sell it. But you find that similar bonds of the same quality and maturity are now paying 9 percent. To

FIGURE 1.1   Treasury Yield Curve

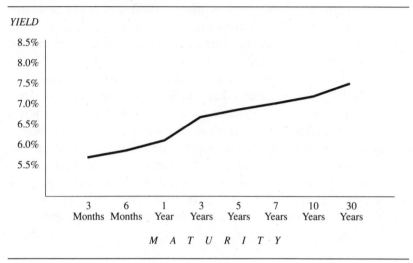

sell, your bond would have to be priced at an amount that would provide a prospective buyer with a 9 percent yield. Thus, you would be able to sell it for approximately $889, since the annual interest of $80 on a bond with a cost of $889 provides a yield of 9 percent ($80 divided by $889).

The yield curve plots the yields of bonds of the same credit quality against their maturity periods, from one month to 30 years. The degree of difference between yields of the shortest and longest maturities, which can also be seen as the premium that investors can expect in return for a long-term commitment, defines the slope of the curve.

While a variety of yield curves are available, the curve most often published in newspapers and financial periodicals tracks Treasury securities. Typically, the yield curve can assume one of three general shapes.

A positive curve indicates that interest offered on longer-term bonds is higher than the rates for short-term bonds. When this occurs, investors with an objective of income might favor longer maturities for a portion of their bond portfolios. A flat curve describes a bond market with a much narrower difference between long- and short-term rates. An inverted curve (also called an abnormal curve) describes the rate situation when short-term rates are higher than long-term. Inverted yield curves occurred in March 1980 and again in March 1989. Figure 1.2 illustrates historical examples of the three types of yield curves with interest rates offered at different maturities and the years in which they occurred.

The yield curve changes continually, due to many factors. These can include Federal Reserve rate hikes, auctions of large blocks of Treasuries, a weak dollar, and investor expectations with respect to future interest-rate movements. If you are an income investor, you can benefit by buying bonds that offer higher yields within the maturity range that matches your expected holding period. If you are seeking capital appreciation in your bond portfolio, and hope to sell bonds at a premium before they mature, you can diversify your selection among various maturities, based on your expectations about interest-rate changes.

FIGURE 1.2   Examples of the Treasury Yield Curve

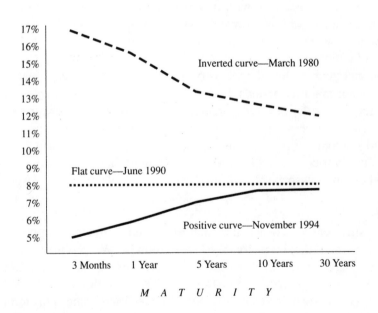

Types of Bonds at a Glance

Bond issuers fall into three categories: (1) corporations; (2) the U.S. government and its agencies; and (3) states, municipalities and other local governments. Each has features and disadvantages you should be aware of when deciding which type of bond best meets your investment needs.

Corporate bonds are issued by corporations to finance their long-term capital projects and are paid back within a specified length of time (called the bond's maturity). To help you in making a judgment about the creditworthiness of a bond, you can check its evaluation by one or more independent rating services. Rating services take a number of factors into consideration, including the issuing company's ability to repay the face value of the bond. We'll look closely at bond ratings in Chapter 8. In general, the interest rate paid reflects the bond's relative safety. Usually, the higher the quality, the lower the interest rate. The interest rate also reflects the bond's maturity: the longer the maturity, the higher the interest paid.

U.S. government bonds can take the form of Treasury securities or securities of certain U.S. agencies, such as those of the Government National Mortgage Association (GNMA)—called "Ginnie Maes." These instruments are backed by the full faith and credit of the U.S. Government as to the timely payment of principal and interest. Other U.S. agency securities, such as the Federal National Mortgage Association—called "Fannie Maes," carry a less formal indirect backing.

Depending on their length of maturity, Treasury issues are designated as U.S. Treasury bills (with maturities from 90 days to one year), U.S. Treasury notes (maturing in one to 10 years) and U.S. Treasury bonds (carrying 10- to 30-year maturities).

Municipal bonds are issued by state and local governments, often to finance specific projects such as highways, schools, recreational facilities, and so on. While they typically pay lower rates than corporate bonds, the interest income is generally exempt from Federal income taxes and frequently from state and local taxes, as well. Thus, a lower yield bond actually can be more attractive than a higher paying taxable security when you figure what the relative tax consequences would be, especially in the higher tax brackets.

Even though less than 1 percent of municipal bonds default, a few well-publicized defaults have resulted in great demand for insured bonds. Demand for insurance is great enough that about 40 percent of new local government issues are insured. See Chapter 3, for an in-depth discussion of municipal bonds.

How Returns Are Calculated

The "total return" of a bond is the change in value of your investment over a particular period, assuming that all interest payments have been reinvested. Two components added together determine a bond's total return:

1. *Yield (interest income).* When you purchase a bond paying $80 interest, for instance, you can expect to receive an annualized yield of 8 percent, the bond's interest income reflected as a percentage of the purchase price.
2. *Capital return.* But yield or interest income is not the only way of determining how profitable your investment has been. While the issuer of a bond promises to pay its face value at maturity, the value of your bond may fluctuate between the issue date and maturity date, usually because of an upward or downward movement in interest rates. Thus, a $1,000 bond coming due in the year 2008 may today be worth $900 or $1,100, depending on whether interest rates in general are higher or lower than the rate paid by your bond. This rise or fall in the value of your principal is known as "capital return."

If a $1,000 bond drops in price to $950, your capital return would be −5 percent. Add that to the bond's 8-percent yield and your total return becomes approximately 3 percent [8% yield + (−5% capital return)]. On the other hand, if your bond rises in price to $1,050, the total return on your bond increases to approximately 13 percent (8% yield + 5% capital return).

Factors Affecting Total Return

Interest Rates.   The first factor that can affect the total return you receive on your fixed-income investment is a change that may take place in interest rates. As noted earlier, generally the market value of bonds move in the opposite direction from interest rates. So, the value of your bonds decline if interest rates go up, and they rise if interest rates go down. *Market risk* is the degree to which a bond's price fluctuates as a result of changes in interest rates.

Maturity.   A bond's maturity also affects how much its value is apt to rise or fall. Bonds with longer maturities usually offer higher yields, but also tend to have more volatile price swings than those with shorter maturities. The longer the life of a bond (its maturity), the greater the degree of price fluctuation. Consequently, more cautious investors typically prefer shorter-term bonds because their exposure to volatility is much less.

Figure 1.3 shows how the prices of bonds with varying maturities would respond following a one percent change in interest rates. As you can see, rising interest rates result in decreasing bond values and vice versa. Further, the degree of volatility increases as maturities lengthen. Note how much more volatility affects the values of long-term bonds than those of intermediate- or short-term bonds.

Credit Quality.   While interest rates and maturity can influence the face value of a bond, a bond's credit quality has an important bearing on its yield. *Credit risk* is the chance that your bond will default (fail to make timely payment of principal and interest). Lower-quality bonds usually offer higher yields but also have a greater risk of default.

FIGURE 1.3   Effect of Interest Rate Changes on Bond Prices

Bond Maturity	Initial Principal of $1,000 and Yield of 10%			
	1% Rise in Rates		1% Decline in Rates	
Short-term (2.5-year maturity)	$979	−2.1%	$1,022	+2.2%
Intermediate-term (7-year maturity)	952	−4.8%	1,051	+5.1%
Long-term (20-year maturity)	920	−8.0%	1,092	+9.2%

Independent rating services evaluate many factors to determine a bond's credit quality, including the issuing company or agency's ability to repay the face value of the bond. Standard & Poor's Corporation and Moody's Investors Service are the two most well-known ratings services that regularly evaluate issuers. They issue ratings that range from the highest quality rating (Aaa for U.S. Treasury securities) to the so-called "junk bonds" of corporations whose financial health may be considered weak.

Just as interest rates and bond values have an inverse relationship, the creditworthiness of an issuer and the interest paid have a similar relationship. For instance, the safest investment you can make, guaranteed by the full faith and credit of the U.S. Government as to the timely payment of principal and interest, usually pays a lower interest rate. As you move down the scale to less creditworthy and, therefore, more speculative bonds, the issuer is forced to pay a higher interest rate to compensate for the greater risk.

Getting Your Bond'$ Worth!

Bonds are an attractive investment because they generally produce a higher and steadier flow of income than you would receive from money market funds or bank savings accounts and the amount invested is usually at less risk than if you had invested it in stocks. Before investing in bonds, though, assess the bonds' market and credit risk to determine whether they are compatible with your personal risk tolerance level.

2

☆ ☆ ☆ ☆ ☆ ☆ ☆ ☆ ☆ ☆ ☆ ☆ ☆ ☆ ☆ ☆ ☆ ☆

Profiting from
U.S. Treasury Bonds

☆ ☆ ☆ ☆ ☆ ☆ ☆ ☆ ☆ ☆ ☆ ☆ ☆ ☆ ☆ ☆ ☆ ☆

Today, interest in U.S. Treasury bonds (Treasuries) has increased because of their high quality and yield compared with other debt securities.

You can buy Treasuries available with a wide range of maturities that can help you satisfy a variety of investment objectives. They are considered among the safest of all investments because payment of interest and principal is guaranteed by the full faith and credit of the U.S. government. Treasuries offer predictable income, which is generally exempt from state and local taxes and repayment of principal in full if held to maturity.

Ample liquidity is available through an active secondary market. The secondary market for Treasuries is the largest such market for any type of security. Through a broker, you have the opportunity to sell your investment prior to maturity or purchase issued securities. As is true with stock and bond investments, your purchases or sales will be subject to prevailing market prices. Prices of Treasury securities will increase as interest rates fall and decrease as rates rise, so you may have a gain or loss if you sell prior to maturity.

How Treasuries Can Help Your Investment Portfolio

Diversification is important in any portfolio. By spreading your investments over different classes of assets, rather than having all your eggs in one basket, you take advantage of a proven investment principle that moderates risk. Most investors with diversified portfolios have a portion of their holdings in bonds and short-term securities. As one of the safest investments available, Treasuries are an attractive investment option. Consider the advantages they offer:

Safety.   Treasuries are considered the safest fixed-income investments, since they are guaranteed by the full faith and credit of the U.S. Government for the prompt payment of interest, and, if you hold your Treasury securities to maturity, you will receive the full face value regardless of market conditions. Your income from Treasury securities is fully predictable for as long as you hold them.

Flexibility.   Treasuries can be ideal investments for either the short or the long term. With the wide range of maturities available and an active secondary market (for ready liquidity), structuring a portfolio is easy and will help you meet investment goals, such as saving for a home down payment, college tuition, or retirement income.

Income.   With Treasuries, a steady stream of interest income will help you meet both short- and long-term needs. The income can be used to supplement retirement income, provide for current expenses, or build an emergency fund. Or, it can be reinvested for capital appreciation through interest compounding.

Tax Advantages.   Although the interest on your Treasury securities is subject to federal taxes, it is *exempt* from state and local taxes. If you live in a state with high income taxes, you may actually keep more of what interest you earn than you would with comparable taxable investments.

Treasury Securities You Can Buy

Short-term *Treasury bills* (T-bills) have 3-, 6-, or 12-month maturities, and are sold at a discount from face value. The difference between the price you pay and the face value you receive at maturity represents your interest earned. *Treasury notes* (T-notes), with 2-, 3-, 5-, or 10-year maturities, and *Treasury bonds* (T-bonds), with 30-year maturity, are medium- to long-term investments that pay interest semiannually. The interest rate you earn on T-notes and T-bonds is locked in at the time of purchase and is not affected by changing market conditions. The rate remains the same until you sell your security or it matures. *Zero-coupon Treasuries* (zeros), also called *STRIPS* (separate trading of registered interest and principal of securities, the Treasury's acronym for its own zero-coupon securities), are sold at deep discounts. Zeros pay no interest during their life; interest is reinvested over the life of the security at the stated rate and paid only at maturity. Even though the interest from zeros isn't available to you until the bond matures, the interest they earn each year is subject to federal income taxes.

Figure 2.1 provides a summary of Treasury securities. Except for zeros, you can buy U.S. Treasury securities at periodic auctions directly from the Federal Reserve (see Chapter 10) or through a broker in the secondary market. Zeros are available in the secondary market only.

FIGURE 2.1 A Summary of U.S. Treasury Securities

Issue	Maturities	Auction Schedule	Minimum Face Value*
T-bills	3 and 6 months	Weekly	$10,000
	1 year	Monthly	10,000
T-notes	2 years	Monthly	5,000
	3 years	Quarterly: Feb., May, Aug., Nov.	5,000
	5 years	Monthly	1,000
	10 years	Quarterly: Feb., May, Aug., Nov.	1,000
T-bonds	30 years	Semi-annually: Feb., Aug.	1,000
Zeros	6 months to 30 years	Available in secondary market only	5,000

* *Thereafter, you can buy in $1,000 increments. Face value is the amount you will receive if the security is held to maturity.*

The Bond Laddering Strategy

To diversify holdings, moderate interest-rate risk, and preserve capital, many investors tailor an investment strategy called *bond laddering*. The idea behind this strategy is to invest in Treasuries with different maturities so that funds become available for reinvestment periodically. This same technique may be used when investing in corporate and municipal bonds.

The following chart gives an example of bond laddering. It shows a 5-year ladder made up of different Treasury issues. In this example, you are investing $50,000 in Treasury securities of varying maturities. This laddered portfolio provides a "blended" (or average) yield of 6.5 percent. Your objectives are achieved by spreading out the maturities over evenly spaced future dates.

Maturity	Interest Rate	Invested Amount
1 year	6.00%	$10,000
2 years	6.25	10,000
3 years	6.50	10,000
4 years	6.75	10,000
5 years	7.00	10,000

Bond laddering can provide you with several advantages:

1. Laddering makes it easy to diversify the maturities of your bond holdings, lessening the effects of uncertainty in a changeable interest-rate environment.

2. During a time of low rates, laddering provides a way to avoid having an entire fixed-income portfolio locked into a set yield for years to come.

3. If rates rise, you can reinvest your maturing bonds at higher rates. If rates fall, you have the protection afforded by the portion of your portfolio that is invested at higher rates.

4. Laddering gives the certainty of having available the principal you need on future dates to meet specific goals. By scheduling maturity dates, you can have the assurance that the funds you're counting on will be available when needed.

U.S. Savings Bonds

Like other Treasury securities, savings bonds are backed by the full faith and credit of the U.S. government, and the interest they pay is exempt from state and local taxes. However, savings bonds have several features that make them quite different from other Treasuries.

Savings bonds can be purchased at any bank, or through your company by payroll deduction, in denominations ranging from as little as $50 to as much as $10,000. The government limits you to investing a maximum of $15,000 in any one year in savings bonds.

Series EE savings bonds pay no coupon interest. Instead, they sell for one-half their face value and are redeemed at full face value upon maturity. In these "accrual-type" bonds, interest is paid when the bond is cashed in on or before maturity and not regularly over the life of the bond. Thus, a $50 bond costs $25 and a $10,000 bond costs $5,000. Federal tax on the accrued interest you have earned is not payable until you redeem the bond.

The interest rate on Series EE Bonds purchased on or after May 1, 1995, is market-based. Bonds held more than five years earn interest equal to 85 percent of the average yield that five-year Treasury securities earned during the period the bond was held. Investors who hold bonds less than five years get a market-based rate equal to 85 percent of the average yield that six-month Treasury bills earned during the bonds' life. No interest is credited on bonds that are held less than six months.

Interest on savings bonds is credited every six months, from the month of purchase. It is important, therefore, that you redeem your EE bonds right after their six-month anniversary. If you redeem prior to that date, you may lose up to several months interest. And here's a money-making tip: Since interest begins to accrue on the first day of the month of purchase, it makes good sense to buy bonds at the end of the month.

For really long-term investors, there is a safety net to protect them against very low interest rates. If a savings bond has not reached face value after 17 years, the Treasury can raise it to that level in a one-time adjustment.

Series HH Bonds are a current income security available at par (purchase price equals face value) in denominations of $500, $1,000,

$5,000, and $10,000. HH bonds are not available for cash purchase but may be obtained in exchange for Series E Bonds, Series EE Bonds and U.S. Savings Notes that are at least 6 months old. They also may be obtained through the authorized reinvestment of matured Series H Bonds. A minimum of $500 in redemption value of older bonds is necessary in order to make an exchange. HH bonds pay interest semiannually at a fixed rate that prevails at the time of exchange (currently 4 percent). That rate is set for the first 10 years that the bond is held and can change when the bond enters an extension period for another 10 years. Interest payments are transmitted by direct deposit to the owner's designated account at a financial institution. You get the interest twice a year and receive your original purchase price at redemption.

Current interest rate information on U.S. savings bonds can be obtained by calling toll-free 800/487-2663.

Getting Your Bond'$ Worth!

U.S. Treasury bonds, among the safest of all investments, are available with a wide range of maturities and can be structured to achieve a variety of investment objectives. They offer predictable income, exemption from state and local taxes, and repayment of principal in full if held to maturity.

3

☆ ☆ ☆ ☆ ☆ ☆ ☆ ☆ ☆ ☆ ☆ ☆ ☆ ☆ ☆ ☆ ☆

Reducing Taxes with Municipal Bonds

☆ ☆ ☆ ☆ ☆ ☆ ☆ ☆ ☆ ☆ ☆ ☆ ☆ ☆ ☆ ☆ ☆

Most investors carefully evaluate yield, safety, and growth potential when they choose an investment. Yet, few stop to consider the
effect of taxes on their investment return. For instance, an investor in
the 36 percent tax bracket could be giving up $36 of every $100 of
investment income to taxes. From a different perspective, if this
investor has an 8 percent income return, it equals just 5.12 percent
after taxes.

Municipal bonds, often called "munis," appeal to investors for two
reasons:

1. *Tax-free income.* Municipal bonds are one of the few remaining
   sources of tax-free income. They provide income that is
   exempt from Federal income taxes, and, in the state of issue,
   municipal bonds are often free from both state and local taxes
   as well. For instance, the state of New York might issue a bond
   to help pay for repaving a tollway, then use the money col-
   lected from the tolls to repay investors. The interest income
   from this bond would be exempt from federal income taxes,
   and for New York residents the interest would also be exempt
   from state and city taxes.

   Income from *some* municipal bonds is subject to the federal
   alternative minimum tax (AMT). AMT is a tax that applies to
   certain high-income investors. Such investors should check to

see if a bond they are considering is subject to AMT before investing.

2. *Diversification.* Bonds have investment characteristics quite different from those of common stocks. Though bond prices are sometimes quite volatile, they are generally considered safer than stocks and can serve to diversify an equity-heavy portfolio. Municipal bonds are generally considered to be high on the investment safety scale, second only to securities issued by the U.S. government and its agencies.

Tax-free investments have been gaining in popularity. According to *Bond Buyer* magazine, over 75 percent of municipal obligations are owned by individual investors through investments in individual bonds and mutual funds. With more than $1.25 trillion of municipal debt outstanding, the sheer size of the tax-free bond market helps to make it stable and liquid, so buying and selling bonds is relatively easy.

What Are Municipal Bonds?

Municipal bonds are interest-bearing securities issued by state and local governments to support their financial needs or to finance public projects. A municipal bond obligates the issuer to pay the bondholder a fixed amount of interest periodically and to repay the principal value of the bond on a specified maturity date. Like bonds issued by corporations or the U.S. government, municipal bonds are considered fixed-income securities, since they offer a steady rate of interest income. They are often called debt obligations, as they represent a loan to the bond issuer.

Types of Municipal Bonds

General obligation (GO) bonds are issued by municipal agencies, such as cities or states, that have taxing authority. Payments of principal and interest on GO bonds are secured by the full faith and credit of the issuer. Thus, the issuing agency promises to use every means available to assure prompt payment of principal and interest, when due.

Revenue bonds are payable from a specific source of income. Sources of income frequently used to pay revenue bond issues include tolls and rents or charges from facilities such as turnpikes, airports, hospitals, and water treatment plants.

The Rewards of Tax-Free Investing

Because the interest from municipal bonds is exempt from federal tax, these securities generally pay lower interest rates than similar taxable investments. Nevertheless, since the interest income is exempt from federal and, in some cases, state and local income taxes, you may actually keep more spendable income from the tax-free security.

Figure 3.1 illustrates the effect of tax-free versus taxable income at different income levels and tax rates. To compare how the two investments might work for you, locate your annual income, after deductions and exemptions, and then read across to find the yield you would need on a taxable investment to match the tax-free yield at various rates. For example, a person in the 31 percent tax bracket must earn 10.14 percent from a fully taxable investment to equal a 7 percent yield that is exempt from federal income tax. With state and local taxes taken into consideration, the difference could be even more dramatic.

FIGURE 3.1 Tax-Free versus Taxable Income

			Assumed Tax-Free Yields					
			5.00%	5.50%	6.00%	6.50%	7.00%	8.00%
Taxable Income		Federal						
Single Return	Joint Return	Tax Rate	Equivalent Taxable Yields					
To $22,750	To $38,000	15%	5.88%	6.47%	7.06%	7.65%	8.24%	9.41%
$22,751–55,100	$38,001–91,850	28%	6.94%	7.64%	8.33%	9.03%	9.72%	11.11%
$55,101–115,000	$91,851–140,000	31%	7.25%	7.97%	8.70%	9.42%	10.14%	11.59%
$115,101–250,000	$140,001–250,000	36%	7.81%	8.59%	9.38%	10.16%	10.94%	12.50%
Over $250,000	Over $250,000	39.6%	8.28%	9.11%	9.93%	10.76%	11.59%	13.25%

The equivalent taxable yields are calculated based on the maximum marginal tax rate at each tax bracket in effect in 1994. These brackets and rates are subject to change. See your tax adviser regarding more recent tax legislation and how tax laws affect your own personal financial situation.

Municipal Bond Investment Risks

As is true with corporate bonds, interest rate risk and credit risk are two major factors you should assess before investing in a municipal bond.

Interest rate risk involves the degree to which a bond's price fluctuates in response to changes in interest rates. Bonds with longer maturities typically offer higher yields but also have the potential for greater price swings than those with shorter maturities.

Credit risk is the chance a bond will default, that is, fail to make timely payment of principal and interest. Lower-quality bonds generally pay higher yields but also have a greater risk of default.

Insured Municipal Bonds

When Orange County, California, filed for bankruptcy in late 1994, it sent shock waves through the investment community. It was the biggest U.S. municipality ever to take that action. One way municipal bond investors can protect themselves from the risk of default is by purchasing triple-A rated insured municipal bonds. The higher credit quality, of course, means you will earn a slightly lower yield. Holders of insured bonds are guaranteed they will continue to receive principal and interest payments on time and in full if their bonds default. Although uninsured Orange County bonds were downgraded after its financial problems became known, triple-A insured bonds were not.

Even though less than 1 percent of local government bonds default, demand for insurance is great enough that about 40 percent of new local government issues are insured, giving them a triple-A rating. Aside from the protection against default, many investors choose insured bonds because the extra protection and triple-A rating insulates them from the uncertainty that sometimes depresses prices and makes it difficult to sell bonds that are involved in controversy even though they have not defaulted.

Major insurers of municipal bonds—all members of the Association of Financial Guaranty Insurors (AFGI)—include AMBAC Indemnity Corporation, Capital Guaranty Insurance Company, Financial Guaranty Insurance Company, Financial Security Assurance Inc., and Municipal Bond Investors Assurance Corporation. Each of these companies' claims-paying ability is rated triple-A by one or more of the major rating agencies. In the 23 years of the bond insurance industry, no investor in a bond insured by an AFGI member company has ever failed to receive a bond payment, and no AFGI-insured bond has ever been downgraded from triple-A.

Getting Your Bond'$ Worth!

Municipal bonds can provide you with one of the few remaining sources of tax-free income. The interest they pay is exempt from federal income taxes and in some cases is exempt from state and local taxes. Furthermore, though sometimes volatile in price, municipal bonds are generally considered more conservative than stocks and can serve to balance an equity-laden portfolio.

4

☆ ☆ ☆ ☆ ☆ ☆ ☆ ☆ ☆ ☆ ☆ ☆ ☆ ☆ ☆ ☆ ☆ ☆

Making Corporate Bonds Work for You

☆ ☆ ☆ ☆ ☆ ☆ ☆ ☆ ☆ ☆ ☆ ☆ ☆ ☆ ☆ ☆ ☆ ☆

If you are seeking investments with a higher rate of return compared to other fixed-income securities, you may want to consider corporate bonds with a wide variety of issues to choose from, including utilities, transportation companies and industrial corporations.

Corporate bonds are debt instruments issued by corporations to raise capital for expansion and other corporate purposes. You, as an investor, lend money to the corporation. The corporation, or the issuer, in turn promises to pay you the principal amount at a preset date. The issuer also promises to make payments of interest to you on a periodic basis, usually every six months. This interest generally is at a fixed rate set when the bond is issued though some bonds are issued where the interest rate may float in relation to the prevailing interest rates until the bond matures.

The corporate bond market is well over $2 trillion, with an active secondary market where securities may be bought and sold through brokers subsequent to original issuance. However, some types of bonds are less actively traded than others, so an investor may have less liquidity.

Corporate Bond Yields

Corporate bonds generally offer higher yields than government Treasury bonds and municipal securities. However, they also carry more risk. Maturities of corporate instruments range from a few weeks to more than thirty years. Interest is typically paid semi-annually. Some corporate bonds are offered as zero-coupon issues, selling at a deep discount from face value. The face value, which represents both principal and accrued interest, is paid at maturity.

Credit Risk

Even though payments to bond investors take precedence over dividend payments to stockholders of a corporation, you, the potential investor, should consider the safety of the issue. The quality of a corporate bond is based on an evaluation of the issuer's financial ability to pay interest and return your principal. Corporate bonds generally have no government backing. If a company files for bankruptcy, your investment may be in jeopardy.

To help determine a bond's creditworthiness, many investors rely on one of two major rating agencies, Moody's Investors Service or Standard & Poor's Corporation, to grade issues in terms of safety. Higher-rated bonds tend to be safer and usually offer a lower yield. Bonds offering higher yields generally have lower credit ratings.

Always check the quality rating of a potential bond investment before you purchase it. And, because the financial health of a company can change, monitoring a corporate bond's rating periodically is important. A change in the quality rating of a bond can affect its liquidity and value. See Chapter 8, How Bonds are Rated for Safety.

Interest Rate Risk

The current yield of a bond moves up or down in response to changes in prevailing interest rates. If interest rates go up, the price of an outstanding bond will go down because any new bond would be issued at the prevailing higher rates. If interest rates go down, the price will go up. Therefore, if you sell a bond early, the price will be subject to the current interest rate environment.

Here's the way it works: Suppose you want to buy an outstanding $1,000 bond that pays $80 per year (an 8 percent yield), but the prevailing interest rate for a comparable newly issued bond has risen to 9 percent. Since you would expect to receive whatever the current interest rate is, in this case 9 percent, you would be willing to pay just $888.89 for the outstanding bond. This is because $80 is 9 percent of $888.89. On the other hand, if interest rates have fallen, so that a comparable bond is yielding 7 percent, you would have to pay $1,142.86 for the outstanding bond (80 = 7 percent of 1,142.86).

If you hold a bond to maturity, of course, you should receive the face value.

Types of Corporate Bonds

Though all corporate bonds are similar in purpose, there are different types. There are five major classifications:

1. *Debenture bonds* are backed by the overall financial health of the company issuing the bond. Since there is no collateral, these bonds represent a greater level of risk and generally offer a higher rate of return.
2. *Collateralized bonds* are backed by assets that the issuer puts up as collateral for the bond. For instance, capital assets backing a bond may include real estate holdings and equipment.
3. *Callable bonds* can be redeemed by the issuer prior to maturity at a predetermined price. They will often offer higher yields than non-callable bonds.
4. *"Sinking fund" bonds* require the issuer to deposit money in a sinking fund with the bond trustee. The sinking fund money is used either to redeem the bond at par prior to maturity or to repay the principal at maturity.
5. *Convertible bonds* can be exchanged by the investor for common stock in the issuing company. This investment offers you the potential for capital appreciation from the underlying common stock. However, because convertibles generally sell at a premium to the conversion value of the stock, these bonds usually offer lower yields than comparable quality nonconvertibles. See Chapter 5, Convertible Bonds, for a full description of this investment opportunity.

Getting Your Bond'$ Worth!

With a market that is well over $2 trillion, corporate bonds continue to be an important investment choice for investors seeking a higher rate of return compared to other fixed-income securities. There is a wide variety of issues to choose from, including utilities, as well as transportation and industrial companies. Corporate bonds generally will offer you higher yields than municipal and Treasury bonds, but they also carry more risk.

5

☆ ☆ ☆ ☆ ☆ ☆ ☆ ☆ ☆ ☆ ☆ ☆ ☆ ☆ ☆ ☆ ☆

Uncovering the Hidden Opportunities in Convertible Bonds

☆ ☆ ☆ ☆ ☆ ☆ ☆ ☆ ☆ ☆ ☆ ☆ ☆ ☆ ☆ ☆ ☆

Many investors could have earned higher returns in recent years, and with less risk, if they had invested in convertible bonds instead of common stocks. A study by Ibbotson Associates, a consulting firm for institutional investors, shows that in the 20 years from 1973 to 1992, convertible bonds provided higher profits than common stocks—with about half as much risk.

Convertible bonds are often overlooked by individual investors because of the hybrid nature of these securities: they are part equity and part bond. Yet the basic principles and terms of convertibles should be as easy to understand as the key concepts of non-convertible securities.

There are four reasons why convertible bonds often outperform common stocks:

1. They offer the safety of bonds.
2. They pay more income than common stocks.
3. They can be converted into common stock, so they share in the rise of the common.
4. Brokerage commissions for bonds are considerably lower than for stocks.

What Is a Convertible Bond?

A convertible bond is a bond that can be exchanged for another security, usually the common stock of the issuing company. Typically, no payment is needed to effect conversion other than the surrender of the bond. The conversion privilege normally lasts for the life of the bond though, in a few cases, the number of common stock shares for which the convertible can be exchanged may change during the life of the convertible.

A convertible bond's value is derived from its conversion privilege (relating to the price of the underlying stock) and from the value it commands simply because it is a bond. Its price rises or falls with its conversion value, that is, with a change in the price of the stock, but its price will normally fall no lower than its *investment value* as an interest-paying bond.

Usually convertible bonds sell at premiums above their conversion and investment values.

Why Buy Convertibles?

Risk-averse investors tend to like convertibles over common stock because they offer several advantages, one of which is greater income. In late 1994, for instance, the average convertible bond provided a yield of nearly 7 percent, while the average dividend-paying stock in the S&P 500 paid less than 3 percent.

Surprisingly, studies (such as the Ibbotson study noted earlier) have shown that convertibles have consistently outperformed common stocks when both income and price appreciation are considered, over periods of five years or more. This is especially noteworthy since convertibles are relatively low in risk. When the stock market falls, not only do convertibles fall less, but they also provide greater income. When the market rises, convertibles do not normally rise in price as fast as common stock, but if the market rise is slow, the greater income from convertibles often causes the total return from convertibles to equal or exceed the total return from common stocks. Only in a rapidly rising stock market do convertibles perform worse.

Another feature that appeals to investors in convertibles is that a portfolio of convertibles will typically be less volatile than a portfolio of common stocks. The more up and down movement there is in the price of a security, the greater the risk that its market value may be low when you need to sell it. Thus, less volatility means lower risk.

Why Convertibles Are Safer, yet More Profitable Than Stocks

Convertibles are lower in risk than stocks for a number of reasons. First, they are a senior security. A company might skip its common stock dividend if earnings decline, but would stop paying bond interest only as a last resort; if interest payments are stopped, bondholders could take control of the company. Second, convertibles almost always pay a higher yield than stocks. The higher yield helps support the price of the bonds even if the price of the stock falls.

Put another way, fairly priced convertibles are always "favorably leveraged." A convertible will be favorably leveraged if it *rises* more on a *rise* in the underlying stock than it falls on a decline in the stock. Convertibles are favorably leveraged because they participate in a rise in the stock, but their higher yields limit the extent of any drop.

Convertible Bond Terms You Should Understand

Conversion ratio is the number of shares of stock for which the convertible can be exchanged. Only the holder of a convertible may convert the issue. The issuing company cannot require the holder to convert or convert it for himself or herself.

Conversion value is the value of a convertible bond if converted into the common stock; it is the price of the common stock multiplied by the bond's conversion ratio. Thus, if you own a bond with a conversion ratio of 25, it is convertible into 25 shares of common stock. If the stock has a market value of $50, the conversion value of your bond is $1,250 (25 x $50).

Premium over conversion value is the percentage by which the price of the convertible bond exceeds the conversion value. For instance, if the price of the convertible is $1,500 and the conversion value is $1,250, the premium over the conversion value is 20 percent.

Investment value is the price at which the convertible would likely trade if it were not convertible. That is, the price at which a "straight" (nonconvertible) bond would trade.

Premium over investment value is the percentage by which the price of the convertible bond exceeds its investment value. For instance, if a convertible bond's price is $1,500 and its investment value (the value the bond would have if it had no conversion feature) is $750 , the premium over investment value is 100 percent.

Call price is the price the convertible may be called at if it is callable. When an issue is called, holders have about 30 days to decide whether or not to convert. A callable bond is one in which the issuing company has the right to redeem the bond prior to maturity. Bonds are most likely called when interest rates decline and conditions are favorable to the issuer.

Call protection means that, from the date of issue, a bond is protected from being called for a period of one or more years. Most convertible bonds are issued with call protection. If you plan to live off the income from a bond or want to hold it for a specific number of years, you should be sure you have call protection because, without it, your bond could be redeemed by the issuer.

Coupon is the interest payment on a bond. Bonds are nearly always issued with a par value of $1,000, the price at which they will be redeemed at maturity. Thus, a bond with a 9 percent coupon pays $90 in interest per year.

"Eurobonds" are bonds that were originally sold overseas, usually by U.S. companies. They trade and pay interest in U.S. dollars. Euro bond interest is usually paid once a year versus domestically issued bonds which pay twice a year.

How To Evaluate Convertibles for Profitability

Corporations issue convertible bonds to raise money. Just like any debt instrument, the issuing company is obligated to pay the coupon rate and repay the face amount at maturity. An exception is zero-coupon bonds which pay no cash interest. They are issued at a discount from the face value, which reflects the accumulation of interest to maturity equal to the stated original yield to maturity.

One distinct feature convertible bonds offer investors is the ability to exchange the bond for the common stock of the issuing company at the holder's option, allowing the investor to participate in the potential appreciation of the underlying common stock while usually receiving a higher yield than the common dividend pays.

Estimating a convertible bond's fair value and determining whether it is currently overvalued or undervalued requires careful consideration of all its features, including the bond's market price, its investment value, its conversion ratio, its conversion value, the price of the underlying common stock, the bond's call price, the premium over conversion value, and the premium over investment value.

A convertible bond's value is drawn both from its conversion privilege and from the value it commands because it's a bond. As its price rises with its conversion value (that is, with a rise in the underlying stock), its price will normally fall no lower than its investment value. Most often, convertibles sell at premiums above both their conversion and investment values. If, on occasion, you are able to buy a convertible at its investment value, you get the conversion privilege free of cost. And if you are able to buy a convertible at its conversion value, you get the investment feature (better quality and generally higher income) free of cost.

An Information Source for Convertible Bond Investing

If you are interested in looking more closely at the investment opportunities available in convertible bonds, consider using *Value Line Convertibles,* a service published by Value Line Publishing, Inc. (220 East 42nd Street, New York, NY 10017-5891; 800-833-0046). The service provides detailed coverage of 585 convertibles, with recommendations, analyses, and performance data. An eight week trial subscription is available.

A Smart Way To Buy Convertible Bonds

You can invest in mutual funds that invest in convertible securities. Such funds seek high income and capital appreciation by investing in a diversified portfolio of bonds, preferred stocks and other securities which are convertible into common stocks. By investing in mutual funds, you automatically obtain professional management, diversification, and low cost to invest. See Chapter 25 for a discussion of mutual funds that specialize in convertible securities.

Getting Your Bond'$ Worth!

Consider convertible bonds to reap higher yields, with less risk, than investments in common stocks. Convertibles offer you the safety of bonds, pay more income than common stocks, and can be converted into common stock, so they share in the potential rise of the common stock.

6

☆ ☆ ☆ ☆ ☆ ☆ ☆ ☆ ☆ ☆ ☆ ☆ ☆ ☆ ☆ ☆ ☆

Growing Your Capital with Zero-Coupon Bonds

☆ ☆ ☆ ☆ ☆ ☆ ☆ ☆ ☆ ☆ ☆ ☆ ☆ ☆ ☆ ☆ ☆

Zero-coupon bonds don't pay out a stream of interest payments like other debt instruments. Instead, they are issued at deep discounts and accumulate and compound the interest. At maturity the full face amount is paid. There are two main attractions of zero-coupon securities for the investor: (1) because of the deep discount, they can be bought at very low prices and (2) the guesswork is removed from interest reinvestment, since the yield to maturity is locked in.

Unless you are used to thinking in terms of compound interest over long periods, the mathematical effects of a zero-coupon bond can seem astonishing. For instance, a $1,000 face amount zero-coupon bond, maturing in 30 years that has a 12 percent interest rate, could be bought today for just $33.50!

Zero-coupon bonds have important disadvantages. Income taxes are payable as interest accrues and, since no current income is derived from the zeros, must come from a different source. The value of zero-coupon bonds tends to be highly volatile. Credit risk of corporate and municipal zeros can be greater than with regular bonds; if an issuer defaults along the way, you will have more to lose since you have not yet received any interest. Finally, inflation can erode the value of the bond at maturity.

When To Use Zero-Coupon Bonds

Taxable zeros are widely purchased for inclusion in tax-deferred accounts, such as IRAs and 401(k) plans. Tax-free zeros are a convenient way for high-taxbracket investors to meet their future goals. They get an after-tax benefit from the lower interest rates of tax-free securities. Zeros often have attractive yields and are normally held until maturity. Their appeal is a locked-in interest rate as opposed to a yield that varies with the reinvestment value of periodic interest payments in a changing market. If you need to sell a zero prior to maturity, like other fixed-income investments, the value will fluctuate inversely with interest rates. If interest rates decline, the value of your zero coupon bond will rise, and if interest rates rise, it will fall.

Types of Zero-Coupon Securities

Corporate zero-coupon bonds are issued by corporations and are not usually recommended for individual investors because of the risk of default and because the yield tends not to be competitive in relation to the risk.

Strips are U.S. Treasury or municipal instruments that *brokerage firms* have separated (stripped) into principal and interest components which are marketed as zero-coupon securities under proprietary acronyms like Salomon Brothers' CATS (Certificates of Accrual on Treasury Securities) and M-CATS (Certificates of Accrual on Tax-exempt Securities). These securities are represented by certificates with the actual securities being held in escrow. The escrow feature assures a high degree of security, although the broker is the actual obligor.

STRIPS (Separate Trading of Registered Interest and Principal of Securities), however, are free of credit risk altogether. STRIPS, the *Treasury's acronym* for its *own* zero-coupon securities, are Treasury bonds issued in the traditional way but separated into interest and principal components at the discretion of bondholders using book entry accounts at Federal Reserve banks.

Municipal zero-coupon securities are issued by state and local governments and are usually exempt from federal taxes and state taxes in the state of issue. Municipal zeros provide a convenient way of providing for the goals of high-tax-bracket investors who get an after-tax benefit from the lower interest rates of municipals.

Zero-coupon convertibles are a fairly recent development. Introduced in the 1980s, these securities come in two types. One, issued with a put option, is convertible into common stock providing growth potential. The other, generally a municipal bond, converts into an interest-paying bond, enabling the holder to lock in a rate of accruing interest, and then, 15 years later, to begin collecting interest payments.

Safety Considerations

The safety of corporate and municipal bonds, unless insured, varies with the credit of the issuer, so it is important to check credit ratings. Treasury issues that are stripped (separated into principal and interest components) by brokerage houses and marketed separately as zero-coupon securities are safe as long as the broker holds the underlying Treasury security in escrow, as is generally done. Some municipal strips, such as M-CATS, are indirectly backed by the U.S. government, since they represent prerefunding invested in Treasury securities. STRIPS, issued directly by the Treasury, are risk-free. Of course, any zero sold in the secondary market prior to maturity are subject to market value fluctuation (interest rate risk).

Getting Your Bond'$ Worth!

You can buy zero-coupon bonds at deep discounts from their face values. Instead of paying out their fixed rate of interest like other debt securities, interest is accumulated and compounded, so you don't have to worry about interest reinvestment. Beware of disadvantages, including current taxability of interest even though it is not being paid out. Also, the value of zero-coupon bonds tends to be highly volatile.

7

☆ ☆ ☆ ☆ ☆ ☆ ☆ ☆ ☆ ☆ ☆ ☆ ☆ ☆ ☆ ☆

How To Use
Money Market Funds

☆ ☆ ☆ ☆ ☆ ☆ ☆ ☆ ☆ ☆ ☆ ☆ ☆ ☆ ☆ ☆

One of the safest and most useful of financial devices, money market funds, get their name from the types of securities in their portfolios: money market securities. Many industrial and financial companies, as well as the federal and local governments, borrow large sums of money for a short period of time (up to one year) by issuing money market securities in exchange for cash. These borrowers are among the most creditworthy institutions in the country. They agree to pay the lender back quickly, with interest.

Money market deposit accounts, offered by banks, are similar to money market mutual funds. But unlike money market mutual funds, which are not federally insured, bank money market deposit accounts carry the same Federal Deposit Insurance Corporation (FDIC) protection afforded other bank accounts. However, the yield is typically lower. For instance, in early 1995, typical bank money market deposit accounts paid slightly over 2 percent, while mutual fund money market accounts offered a rate in excess of 5 percent.

The various institutions that borrow in the short-term money market use a few different kinds of instruments. The federal government borrows by way of Treasury bills (T-bills) and federal agency notes (T-notes), major corporations borrow by way of IOUs called commercial paper, and banks issue large certificates of deposit (CDs) and make agreements to repurchase government securities.

These are the types of instruments taxable money market funds hold in their portfolios. Tax-exempt money market funds invest in bonds with short maturities issued by states and municipalities to finance public projects. Money market funds limit the average maturity of their portfolios to 90 days or less. The average maturity for most funds is about 50 days.

Because money market mutual funds lend money for only brief periods of time to the borrowing institutions, the risk of loss in a money market fund portfolio is slight. So, most money market funds manage their portfolios with the aim of holding their *net asset value* (NAV, the price at which you buy and sell shares) constant at $1 per share with no sales charge or fee to buy or sell. In contrast, the NAV in other types of mutual funds rises and falls with the values of the securities in their underlying portfolios fluctuate.

The constant NAV of a money market fund makes it one of the safest investments available. Although it is not insured, chances are remote that you would lose any of your principal (the initial amount of money you invest) in a money market fund. As an indication of the esteem in which they are held, by early 1995 there were well over 21 million shareholder accounts in taxable money market funds in the United States, with assets in excess of $460 billion.

How You Can Use Money Market Funds

You can use money market funds in four main ways:

1. A place to park your money between financial transactions until you decide which savings or investment choice to take;
2. A savings account when financial circumstances or economic conditions make other investment options look too risky;
3. A cash management account where you can earn market rates on the money you use for ordinary bill payment; and
4. A source of tax-free income when you invest in tax-exempt money market funds

Many people use their money market fund as a permanent savings account. They add to it periodically for other purposes such as when they need a financial parking place or want to save for a specific purchase.

The Yield on Money Market Funds

Money market funds receive interest payments from the financial institutions, government agencies, and corporations to which they lend money. These payments are passed through to you in the form of dividends. Most money market funds credit dividends to your account every business day and pay them monthly. You can automatically reinvest these dividends in additional shares of the fund, or receive them in cash. Reinvesting your dividends puts more money to work for you, increasing your earning power.

Yield is a measure of the rate of return on your investment, expressed as a percentage. You can compare yields easily among money market funds because all funds calculate their yields in the same way, as prescribed by the Securities and Exchange Commission (SEC). Most metropolitan newspapers list yields every week for many of the more than 650 taxable money market funds.

Yields are tied to money market rates and may change from day to day, and, of course, yields for past periods cannot predict future yields. Since the dividends you receive are based on the interest payments made to your fund, when interest rates go up, so will yields. When interest rates go down, yields will go down, too.

When you invest in a money market fund, you are buying shares of the fund. Each share represents ownership in all the fund's underlying assets. Dividends are paid out in proportion to the number of shares you own. So, whether you invest just a few hundred dollars or hundreds of thousands of dollars, you get the same yield per dollar invested.

Liquidity

One of the great advantages of a money market fund, like that of any other type of mutual fund, is that your investment is liquid (it can easily be converted into cash). By law, money market funds must stand ready to buy back (redeem) your shares on any business day. If you need to cash in all or part of your money market shares, the fund will issue a check to you. In many cases you can arrange for the fund to wire the money to your bank account.

A convenience offered by most mutual funds is the checkwriting privilege, by which you can pay personal bills and obligations directly from your fund account. Typically, there is a minimum amount for checks, $250 or $500. Checkwriting makes it possible for you to accumulate earnings on money that you use for paying household expenses.

Tax-Exempt Money Market Funds

Investors have more than $100 billion in tax-exempt money market funds. These funds offer all the advantages of taxable funds plus earnings that are generally exempt from federal taxation; for some high-tax-bracket taxpayers, a portion of the income may be subject to the federal alternative minimum tax.

To generate tax-exempt income, these funds only invest in short-term municipal bonds issued by states and municipalities to finance public projects and other tax-exempt securities with short remaining maturities. Because of the extra benefit provided by tax exemption, yields on tax-exempt funds are generally lower than taxable money market yields. For example, in early 1995, a typical taxable money market fund yielded 5.12 percent, while a comparable tax-exempt fund yielded 3.35 percent.

Single-state funds, also known as double tax-exempt funds, invest only in the short-term municipal bonds of one state. Residents of that state who invest in these funds will receive earnings that are exempt from both federal and state taxation.

How To Invest in Money Market Funds

One way to choose a money market fund is by obtaining a copy of *Directory of Mutual Funds,* a publication of the Investment Company Institute (1401 H Street, Suite 1200, Washington, DC 20005; 202-326-5800). The Institute is the national association of mutual funds; its directory lists all types of funds, with separate sections on money market funds. The annual directory, available at low cost, provides each fund's address, phone number, minimum initial and subsequent investment amounts, and information on where to buy shares.

You can invest by calling the fund of your choice (most have toll-free 800 numbers) and asking for an application form along with a prospectus. To open an account, just complete and return the form with your check.

Getting Your Bond'$ Worth!

Use money market funds to park your money between financial transactions, as a savings account when financial circumstances or economic conditions make other investment options look too risky, as a cash management account where you can earn market rates on the money you use for ordinary bill payment, and as a source of tax-free income, when you invest in tax-exempt money market funds.

8

☆ ☆ ☆ ☆ ☆ ☆ ☆ ☆ ☆ ☆ ☆ ☆ ☆ ☆ ☆ ☆

How Bonds Are
Rated for Safety

☆ ☆ ☆ ☆ ☆ ☆ ☆ ☆ ☆ ☆ ☆ ☆ ☆ ☆ ☆ ☆

If you're safety conscious, it generally doesn't pay to invest in lower-quality bonds. Stick with high-quality investments. For the utmost credit safety, choose U.S. Treasury obligations. The next safest are U.S. government agency obligations. There are also many top-quality corporate and municipal bonds that are "investment-grade" and considered very safe. Avoid money market funds investing in below-top-tier instruments and bonds that are below investment-grade (junk bonds) unless you understand and are willing to accept the risks.

Most corporate and many municipal bonds carry a letter coded rating to indicate their relative credit quality. Mutual funds that include corporate or municipal bonds and other debt instruments in their portfolios specify the credit quality of bonds they are permitted to invest in. Rating systems have been developed by several widely recognized investment services, and many bonds, but not all, are evaluated by these services to determine the probability of default by the issuers.

Standard & Poor's Corporation, Moody's Investors Service, Inc., Duff & Phelps, and Fitch's Investors Service are the major firms that analyze the financial strength of each bond's issuer, whether a corporation or a government body. Bonds are assigned ratings by these firms to assist in determining the suitability of a particular instrument for investment purposes. For example, Standard & Poor's classifies investment-grade bonds as AAA, AA, A, and BBB. Anything lower is speculative; institutions that invest other people's money may not, under most state laws, buy them.

Since an issuer pays a substantial cost to obtain a rating by one of these services, debt securities are often issued on an unrated basis. This is particularly true if the total value of the offering is deemed insufficient to justify the cost of obtaining a rating. So, the fact that a bond issue is unrated does not by itself necessarily indicate that it is an unsound investment.

CORPORATE BONDS

Below is a brief description of the corporate bond rating system used by Moody's Investors Service, which is somewhat similar to Standard & Poor's (used with permission).

Moody's Investors Service, Inc.

Aaa—Bonds rated Aaa are judged to be of the best quality. They carry the smallest degree of investment risk and are generally referred to as "gilt-edge." Interest payments are protected by a large or exceptionally stable margin and principal is secure. Though the various protective elements are likely to change, potential changes are most unlikely to impair the fundamentally strong position of such issues.

Aa—Bonds rated Aa are judged to be of high quality by all standards. Together with the Aaa group they constitute what are generally known as high-grade bonds. They are rated lower than the best bonds because margins of protection may not be as large as those for Aaa securities; there may be greater fluctuation of protective elements, or other elements may be present that make the long-term risks appear somewhat larger than those in Aaa securities.

A—Bonds rated A possess many favorable investment attributes and are considered upper-medium-grade obligations. Factors giving security to principal and interest are considered adequate, but elements may be present that suggest a susceptibility to impairment sometime in the future.

Baa—Bonds rated Baa are considered medium-grade obligations, i.e., they are neither highly protected nor poorly secured. Interest payments and principal security appear adequate for the present, but certain protective elements may be lacking or may be characteristically unreliable over any great length of time. Such bonds lack outstanding investment characteristics and, in fact, have speculative characteristics as well.

Ba—Bonds rated Ba are judged to have speculative elements. Their future cannot be considered assured. Often the protection of interest and principal payments may be moderate and, therefore, not sufficiently secure during both good and bad times over the future. Uncertainty of position characterizes bonds in this class.

B—Bonds rated B generally lack characteristics of the desirable investment. Assurance of interest and principal payments or maintenance of other terms of the contract over any long period of time may be small.

Caa—Bonds rated Caa are of poor standing. Such issues may be in default, or elements of danger may exist with respect to principal or interest.

Ca—Bonds rated Ca represent obligations that are highly speculative. Such issues are often in default or have other marked shortcomings.

C—Bonds rated C are the lowest-rated class of bonds, and issues can be regarded as having extremely poor prospects of ever attaining any real investment standing.

Moody's applies the numerical modifiers 1, 2 and 3 in each generic rating classification from Aa through B in its corporate bond rating system. The modifier 1 indicates that the security ranks in the higher end of its generic rating category, 2 indicates a midrange ranking, and 3 indicates that the issue ranks in the lower end.

MUNICIPAL BONDS

As is the case with debt securities issued by corporations, credit risk should be considered in connection with bonds issued by states and municipalities. An investor who buys individual tax-free securities or tax-free mutual fund shares should be concerned about the possibility that a bond issuer will fail to make timely payments of interest or principal to a portfolio. The credit risk of a portfolio depends on the credit quality of its underlying securities. In general, the lower the credit quality of a portfolio's municipal securities, the higher a portfolio's yield, all other factors (such as maturity) being equal.

Below is a brief description of the municipal bond rating system used by Moody's Investors Service (used with permission).

Moody's Investors Service

Aaa—Bonds rated Aaa are judged to be the best quality and carry the smallest degree of investment risk.

Aa—Bonds rated Aa are judged to be of high quality by all standards.

A—Bonds rated A possess many favorable investment attributes and are considered high medium-grade issues.

Baa—Bonds rated Baa are considered medium-grade issues.

Ba—Bonds rated Ba are judged to have speculative elements. Future payment of interest and principal cannot be well assured.

NR—Not rated.

MIG 1—Short-term tax-exempt debt instruments of the best quality with strong protection are given the rating MIG 1.

Prime 1—Prime 1 is the designation given to commercial paper of the highest quality.

Getting Your Bond'$ Worth!

To reduce credit risk when buying bonds, include only investment-grade (BBB or better) bonds in your portfolio; lower-rated debt securities are considered speculative. If you're safety conscious and want the utmost credit safety, choose U.S. Treasury obligations.

9

☆ ☆ ☆ ☆ ☆ ☆ ☆ ☆ ☆ ☆ ☆ ☆ ☆ ☆ ☆ ☆

Start with a
Financial Plan

☆ ☆ ☆ ☆ ☆ ☆ ☆ ☆ ☆ ☆ ☆ ☆ ☆ ☆ ☆ ☆

Fixed-income investments represent the largest securities market in the United States, far larger than the stock market. While stocks traded on U.S. exchanges represent some $4 trillion in value, the value of fixed-income investments is more than $11 trillion!

Why Invest?

Most of us invest in order to secure our financial future. But having decided to invest, we are faced with some complex choices. Are we investing for current income? For future income? For capital growth?

The popularity of fixed-income securities is easy to understand. They provide four important investment objectives:

1. *They are safe.* If your goal is capital preservation, you can choose government-backed securities or short-term securities with minimum volatility and maximum access to your money.
2. *They can provide regular income.* You can choose securities that pay a fixed amount of interest at regular intervals.
3. *They offer diversification and growth.* Fixed-income securities can provide asset diversification in equity-heavy portfolios. And when interest rates fall, the prices of fixed-income securities

rise, offering the potential for capital gains. But remember, prices fall when rates rise.

4. *They can save taxes.* Some fixed-income securities are exempt from federal taxes, some from state taxes, and some from both.

While this book is concerned primarily with bond investments, the extraordinary volatility of the securities markets continues to remind us of the importance of sensible portfolio planning for long-term investment success.

Do you invest and wonder whether you have the right mix of investments for your personal situation? This chapter can help. It is designed to help you sort through the variety of current individual security and mutual fund offerings, guiding you to develop a well-designed plan for investing.

Plan for the Long Term

A financial plan focuses on your long-term investments, commitments generally made for five years or more. Top priority objectives for most investors are retirement and college funding. "Investing" means taking a calculated degree of risk with your money in pursuit of higher returns than is possible with "saving," where safety and conservatism are paramount concerns. Interim declines will occur in the value of your investments. The ideas in this chapter are for investors with the patience to ride out short-term declines in the bond markets in pursuit of potentially higher returns.

Short-Term Needs

Before you begin your investment program, take care of your short-term needs with a savings program. Short-term goals are monies you may need within five years. Needs would include an emergency or "rainy day" fund, or savings for a car, home, or another major purchase. An emergency fund of three to six months' worth of living expenses is generally reasonable (up to a year's worth if you are self-employed or retired). Add to that savings for other short-term goals.

Short-term savings should be invested where they are safe and accessible. Popular choices are money market funds and certificates of deposit (CDs). Bank CDs pay a fixed rate of interest and your principal is guaranteed by an agency of the U.S. government, but you are subject to a penalty for early withdrawal. Money market fund yields fluctuate and do not carry a guarantee, but your money is available at any time with no penalties. Short-term bond funds provide another option. They typically carry a somewhat higher yield, but are subject to some market fluctuation.

Asset Classes

The most critical step in a long-term investment program is to develop an asset allocation. Your asset allocation is the balance you have among three investment classes: cash reserves, bonds, and common stocks.

Cash reserve securities provide a stable investment value and current interest income. Money market funds, bank CDs, and U.S. Treasury bills are included in this category.

Bonds are interest-bearing debt securities issued by the Federal government and its agencies, state and local governments, and corporations. Bonds typically offer higher yields than cash reserves, but their value fluctuates with market conditions.

Common stocks represent ownership rights in a corporation, usually pay dividends and offer the potential for capital growth, but stock market risk can be substantial.

Your future investment returns depend largely on how you divide your money among these classes, not so much on the particular cash reserve, bond, or common stock investments you choose.

Investment Returns

According to Ibbotson Associates, common stocks have produced the highest average annual returns over the long term (approximately 10 percent per year since 1926), bonds were next at 5 percent, followed by cash reserves at less than 4 percent. The advantage of stocks for long-term growth of capital is compelling. Over the last 30 years, a typical investment of $10,000 in a portfolio of common stocks would have grown to more than $197,000, bonds to $84,000 and cash reserves to

$69,000. During this period, stocks outperformed bonds and cash reserves by more than two to one, illustrating the power of compounding—the cumulative impact of investment returns over time.

Risk

There is a risk/reward tradeoff in achieving investment returns: in order to pursue higher returns, you must be willing to assume additional risk. Stocks and bonds offer a higher returns than cash reserves, but they also expose you to higher degrees of risk.

If you own individual stocks and bonds, you are exposed to *specific risk*—the risk that problems with an individual company or bond issuer will cause the value of your investment to fall dramatically. Specific risk largely can be eliminated through diversification (conveniently through the use of mutual funds). Spreading your money among many stocks and bonds will greatly reduce the impact of a single security.

Diversification reduces the risk of loss from a single investment, but two other important risks remain:

Market risk is the risk that the stock or bond markets will decline in value. The stock market is influenced by investors' changing expectations for the economy and individual companies. The bond market is affected by expectations about interest rates and inflation. Both markets are swayed by emotional factors, such as hope and fear.

Inflation risk exposes you to a reduction in the real value of your investment because of a general increase in the cost of living. If your investment earns 8 percent, but inflation is 3 percent, your "real" return is just 5 percent.

Common Stock versus Bond Risk

Market risk with common stocks can be substantial. For instance, a money market fund might earn 5 percent per year, but stocks can rise or fall by that amount in a single day. A severe market drop can be much worse. In October 1987, stock prices fell 20 percent in one day. A *bear market* is when stock prices decline over an extended period; a *bull market* is an extended period of rising stock prices. In the worst bear market in recent times, from 1973 to 1974, a diversified portfolio of stocks fell by 37 percent.

With stock investments, interim losses are inevitable. It took many investors four years to recover their losses after the bear market of 1973 to 1974 (assuming reinvestment of dividends). After the great crash of 1929, it took eight years for the average investment to return to its original value.

The bond market is generally less risky than the stock market, although there have been times, such as the late 1970s and 1993–1994, when some bonds were just as risky as stocks.

Bond prices are tied to prevailing interest rates in the economy. As interest rates fall, bond prices rise. When rates rise, prices fall. The extent of a bond's rise or fall depends on its maturity; the longer the maturity of a bond, the greater its sensitivity to interest rates. Short-term bonds, those maturing in two to five years, are the least risky. Intermediate-term bonds, with maturities of five to ten years, have greater price fluctuations. Long-term bonds, maturing in more that ten years, experience the greatest price swings. A 30-year bond tends to be very volatile.

How Time Affects Market Risk

Both the stock and bond markets can be risky over a short period, but time has a moderating effect on market risk. The longer you hold a stock or bond investment, the less your chance of losing money, and the greater your chance of earning a return close to the long-term average.

Studies have shown that a one-year investment in stocks historically has produced returns ranging from −43.3 percent to +53.9 percent. Over ten-year periods, however, returns have varied from −0.9 percent per year for the worst periods to +20.1 percent for the best ten years. So, while risk can be substantial over short time frames, over longer periods, the chance of losing money and your exposure to market risk are much less. The same principle applies to bonds, though bonds are less risky than stocks.

Inflation Risk over Time

Inflation represents a significant threat to even a well- diversified portfolio of securities. Historically, the annual inflation rate has averaged just over 3 percent, offsetting most of the returns from cash reserves and bonds. However, inflation has offset less than half the return from common stocks, giving stocks the reputation of an "inflation hedge," a way to protect your money against the ravages of inflation.

Allocating Your Assets

In building a long-term investment program, your first step is to determine an asset allocation, that is, a plan on how to divide your savings among cash reserves, bonds, and stocks.

The way you allocate your assets depends on four factors: your objectives, your time horizon, your ability to tolerate risk, and your financial situation. Time is particularly important; the longer you have to invest, the greater the risk you can assume.

If you are investing for retirement, to a build a college fund, or for some other long-term purpose, your objective is to accumulate assets. Thus, your asset allocation should emphasize growth. In later years, your objectives will include preserving the money you have accumulated and spending it to support your standard of living. Your investments should emphasize income, with some capital growth to offset inflation.

Based on these objectives and your time horizon, your asset allocation might emphasize stocks when you are young, and bonds and cash reserves when you are older. Figure 9.1 offers guidelines for allocation at different ages, and assumes you retire in your early 60s. The chart applies only to your long-term investment money. You should also have a separate savings fund for emergencies and other short-term goals.

After you have decided how to allocate your assets, two other factors should be considered: your tolerance for risk and your personal financial situation. These factors may influence you to modify the asset allocation model you have chosen.

FIGURE 9.1 Allocation of Assets at Different Ages

Your Age and Objective	Recommended Asset Allocation
20–49 Growth	80% Stocks 20% Bonds
50–59 Balanced growth	60% Stocks 40% Bonds
60–74 Conservative growth	40% Stocks 40% Bonds 20% Cash reserves
75 and over Income	20% Stocks 60% Bonds 20% Cash reserves

A low *tolerance for risk* may mean you are not prepared to see your investments fluctuate in value. The asset allocations suggested above assume you are willing to tolerate short-term ups and downs in the stock and bond markets in the pursuit of higher returns over time. There is no simple way to measure your tolerance level for short-term fluctuations in the value of your investments. Some investors learn their tolerance for risk only after owning securities for a time and experiencing actual fluctuations in value. Very conservative investors may decide to avoid stocks altogether.

How you feel about your *financial situation* is the final factor to consider in asset allocation. If you feel constrained or limited in your personal finances, you may opt toward a lower-risk allocation. A sound financial situation may influence you to adopt a more aggressive stance.

Implementing Your Plan

An important issue to consider is *when* to make your investments. Many investors hesitate when it comes time to invest, fearing market fluctuations. It can be disheartening when beginning an investment program to have your first investment drop in value because of a "market correction." In an attempt to solve this problem, some investors adopt a "market timing" strategy, hoping to invest when prices are low and sell when prices are high.

"Buy low, sell high." This sounds great in theory. The problem is that few investors, if any, can accurately foresee the direction of the securities markets. The problem with market timing is that market rallies typically occur in brief spurts. More often than not, market timers are "out of the market" when prices rise, and the rally is over before they invest in hopes of benefiting from the rise.

One strategy for avoiding the pitfalls of market timing is "constant dollar investing", also known as dollar-cost-averaging. With constant dollar investing, you invest a certain dollar amount at regular intervals, regardless of market conditions. This strategy lets market fluctuations work for you, not against you. When prices are low, you buy more shares with your regular investment. When prices rise, you buy fewer shares. Because you buy more shares when prices are lower, the average cost of your shares will generally be below the average price of those shares over the period you are investing.

Constant dollar investing works well when you are putting aside money from your current income. But what do you do if you receive a large lump sum of money, say from an inheritance or pay-out from an employer-sponsored retirement plan? Should you invest it all at once, or invest it over time using the constant dollar plan?

If the lump sum was previously invested in stocks and bonds, it makes sense to put it back to work immediately once you receive it. On the other hand, if the lump sum was previously invested in cash reserves, you have two choices. You can put the entire sum to work in accordance with your asset allocation plan and take the risk that the markets may drop. If you feel uncomfortable about the risk of a short-term market reversal, you can gradually move the money into the securities of your choice using the constant dollar investment plan. With constant dollar investing, you forfeit potentially higher returns in rising markets, but you also reduce your exposure to market downturns.

Remember, though, constant dollar investing cannot assure a profit or protect against a loss in declining markets. But a commitment to a long-term constant dollar investing program does reduce the chances of investing at the "top" of the bond or stock markets.

Getting Your Bond'$ Worth!

Take a disciplined, systematic approach to investing. Focus on your long-term investments, commitments generally made for five years or more. Whether you are buying individual securities or mutual funds, the most critical step in a long-term investment program is to develop an asset allocation, the balance you have among cash reserves, bonds and common stocks.

10

☆ ☆ ☆ ☆ ☆ ☆ ☆ ☆ ☆ ☆ ☆ ☆ ☆ ☆ ☆ ☆ ☆ ☆

How To Buy
U.S. Treasury Securities
Directly

☆ ☆ ☆ ☆ ☆ ☆ ☆ ☆ ☆ ☆ ☆ ☆ ☆ ☆ ☆ ☆ ☆ ☆

It's a lot easier than you think to buy U.S. Treasury securities, the safest investments money can buy. These securities are direct obligations of the U.S. government. Contrary to what your banker or broker might tell you, buying Treasury bills, notes or bonds directly from the Federal Reserve is easy. And you can invest in Treasuries without paying any commissions, fees, or other charges through a system called "Treasury Direct."

Types of Treasury Securities

The Treasury issues three types of marketable securities: bills, notes, and bonds. When originally issued, they are sold through an auction process. They are referred to as marketable securities because after their original issue they are bought and sold in the secondary (commercial) market at prevailing market prices through financial institutions, brokers, and dealers in investment securities.

The essential distinction between a bill, note and bond is the length of time, or term, the security will be outstanding from the date of the issue. Treasury bills are short-term obligations issued with a term of one year or less. Treasury notes are medium-term obligations issued with a term of at least one year but not more than ten years. Treasury bonds are long-term obligations issued with a term greater than ten years. The Treasury announces the issue date and maturity date with each new issue of a bill, note and bond.

Treasury bills are different in that they do not bear a stated rate of interest as do notes and bonds. Bills are sold at a discount from par. The owner does not receive any interest payments during the life of the instrument. The difference between the purchase price of the bill and the amount which the owner is paid at maturity (par), or when the bill is sold prior to maturity, represents the interest on the bill. Treasury notes and bonds bear a stated rate of interest and the owner receives semi-annual interest payments.

Marketable Treasury securities are not redeemable before maturity unless, by the terms of their issue, they are callable. If called, they stop earning interest on the date called. You are informed at the time of purchase if your securities are subject to call.

Marketable Treasury securities are issued only in book-entry form at original issue. Book-entry securities are represented by accounting entries maintained electronically on the records of the Treasury, a Federal Reserve Bank or Branch, or financial institution. Certificates are no longer offered at original issue.

Treasury Direct

If you elect to invest in Treasury bills, notes, or bonds by using the Treasury Direct Book-entry Security System, you may purchase the securities at original issue through any Federal Reserve Bank or Branch. The Treasury Direct system is designed primarily for investors who plan to retain their securities from the issue date to maturity. However, you may arrange through a bank or brokerage firm for your investment to be sold before maturity. This is done by requesting that your securities held in the Treasury Direct system be transferred to the commercial system. Your request must be made at least 20 days before an interest payment date or the maturity date of the security.

A listing of the 37 Treasury Direct Servicing Offices at the Federal Reserve Banks and Branches, and Bureau of the Public Debt where you can purchase Treasury securities has been included at the end of this chapter. You can make your transactions in person or by mail.

You can establish a single Treasury Direct account for all eligible marketable Treasury securities. After setting up an account, you will receive a statement of account in Treasury Direct and whenever transactions occur within your account. Principal and interest payments from a Treasury Direct account are paid electronically by direct deposit into your account in a locally authorized bank or other financial institution.

Offering Schedule of Treasuries

Bills

Three series of Treasury bills are offered on a regular basis. Two series of bills, one having a 13-week and the other a 26-week term, are offered each week. Unless holidays or special situations occur, the pattern of weekly bill issues is as follows:

1. the offering is announced on Tuesday;
2. the bills are auctioned the following Monday; and
3. the bills are issued on the Thursday following the auction.

Bills with a 52-week term are usually offered every four weeks as follows:

1. the offering is announced on Friday;
2. the bills are auctioned the following Thursday; and
3. the bills are issued on the Thursday following the auction.

When a normal auction date is a holiday, the auction may be held on the business day preceding or following the holiday.

Notes and Bonds

Though the schedule for the sale of notes and bonds may vary, the Treasury generally observes the following schedule:

1. two-year notes and five-year notes are issued on the last business day of each month;

2. three-year notes and ten-year notes are issued every three months on the 15th of February, May, August and November; and

3. 30-year bonds are issued on the 15th of February and August.

Announcements of all offerings of original issue are made through press releases and carried in major newspapers and wire services.

Bill Sales Procedures

The minimum dollar amount acceptable for a tender (application) for Treasury bills is $10,000. Tenders for more than $10,000 must be in multiples of $1,000. Tenders may be submitted competitively or noncompetitively. Competitive bidders must submit tenders on a discount rate basis with two decimals, such as 4.25 percent. Common fractions may not be used. Competitive bidders may have their bids rejected or may pay a higher price for the security than the noncompetitive price. If you are interested in being a competitive bidder, contact one of the Federal Reserve Servicing Offices listed at the end of this chapter for further information.

If, like most investors, you submit a noncompetitive bid, you agree to pay the price equivalent to the weighted discount rate of accepted competitive tenders. In the auction process for bills, all noncompetitive tenders are accepted. Noncompetitive tenders from any single bidder may not exceed $1 million.

The auction results provide information about the range of accepted discount rates and their equivalent prices and investment rates. The discount rate is based on the par value of the bills, while the investment rate is based on the purchase price of the bills and reflects the actual yield to maturity. Both rates are calculated on the actual number of days to maturity. The discount rate is calculated on a 360-day basis (twelve 30-day months). The investment rate is calculated on a 365-day basis.

Note and Bond Sales Procedures

Treasury notes and bonds are sold at a minimum of $1,000 and in multiples of $1,000. The exception is notes with terms of less than four years, which are sold at a minimum of $5,000 and in multiples of $1,000. The specific terms of each new issue, including the minimums available, are provided in the offering announcement. Noncompetitive tenders from any single bidder may not exceed $5 million.

The auction for notes and bonds is done on a yield basis, which means that the competitive bidding is on the yield the investor is welling to accept on the security. Therefore, if you bid 5.82 percent, it means you will accept an annual yield of 5.82 percent as the return on your investment.

In the auction process for notes and bonds, all noncompetitive tenders are accepted. As in the sale of Treasury bills, most individual investors submit noncompetitive bids. Competitive bidders may have their bids rejected or may pay a higher price than the noncompetitive price.

When the price of the security is less than par, the investor will receive a discount, which is the difference between the purchase price and par. When the price is over par, the investor will be required to pay a premium, which is also the difference between par and the purchase price. While a discount or premium does affect the return to an investor, it does not affect the stated interest rate the Treasury will pay investors on an annual basis.

In some cases, the investor may be required to pay accrued interest if the security pays interest income for a period prior to the issue date. When the security is announced for sale, the terms will specify if payment of accrued interest is required.

How To Invest Through Treasury Direct

To purchase Treasury securities through Federal Reserve Banks and Branches, you should complete a Treasury Direct tender form. Tender forms are available at any Federal Reserve Bank or Branch, or at the Bureau of the Public Debt. They may be obtained by mail or in person. When you submit your tender form by mail, the notation "Tender for Treasury (Bill, Note or Bond)" should be printed at the bottom of the envelope in which it is sent.

Your tender must be received at the Federal Reserve Bank or Branch, or at the Bureau of the Public Debt by the deadline established in the public announcement. Noncompetitive tenders submitted by mail will be considered timely if they are postmarked no later than the day prior to the auction and are received by the issue date.

How To Pay

The tender must be signed and submitted with full payment to the servicing Federal Reserve Bank or Branch, or for investors living in the Washington, D.C., metropolitan area, to the Bureau of the Public Debt. Payment may be made in any of the following ways:

1. with checks issued by banks, savings and loan associations, or credit unions, or by personal checks (Note: No two-party checks will be accepted. Personal checks submitted in payment for Bills must be certified.);
2. by cash (U.S. currency) presented in person; or
3. by Treasury securities maturing on or before the issue date.

Reinvestment or Redemption

Securities held in Treasury Direct are paid at maturity by direct deposit, unless you have elected to reinvest the proceeds of the maturing securities into new securities.

A request for reinvestment of Treasury bills, for a period of up to two years, may be made on the tender at the time of original purchase. Reinvestment for notes and bonds held in Treasury Direct are not available at original issue. However, owners of bills, notes or bonds not scheduled for reinvestment are sent a pre-redemption notice which shows the eligible securities, if any, into which reinvestments are possible. If you wish to reinvest a security, the notice must be completed and returned by the date specified in the notice.

Taxation

Treasury securities are subject to all federal taxes, such as income tax, estate, gift or excise taxes. However, interest earned on Treasury securities is exempt from state and local income taxes. The interest on bills, which are bought with the interest discounted, is taxable in the year in which the bills mature or are sold.

Where To Buy Treasuries

Call, write, or visit in person any of the following 37 Treasury Direct Servicing Offices located at Federal Reserve Banks and Branches, and the Bureau of the Public Debt, throughout the country to obtain a tender. No matter where you are or where you move, you can contact the Servicing Office nearest you to make transactions and receive information on your account.

FIGURE 10.1 Federal Reserve Banks and Branches

FRB Atlanta
Securities Service Dept.
104 Marietta Street
Atlanta, GA 30303
404-521-8653

FRB Baltimore
P.O. Box 1378
502 South Sharp Street
Baltimore, MD 21203
410-576-3300

FRB Birmingham
P.O. Box 830447
1801 Fifth Avenue, North
Birmingham, AL 35283-0447
205-731-8708

FRB Boston
P.O. Box 2076
600 Atlantic Avenue
Boston, MA 02106
617-973-3810

FRB Buffalo
P.O. 961
160 Delaware Avenue
Buffalo, NY 14240-0961
716-849-5000

FRB Charlotte
P.O. Box 30248
530 East Trade Street
Charlotte, NC 28230
704-358-2100

FRB Chicago
P.O. Box 834
230 South LaSalle Street
Chicago, IL 60690
312-322-5369

FRB Cincinnati
P.O. Box 999
150 East Fourth Street
Cincinnati, OH 45201
513-721-4787 Ext. 334

FIGURE 10.1, Continued. Federal Reserve Banks and Branches

FRB Cleveland
P.O. Box 6387
1455 East Sixth Street
Cleveland, OH 44101
216-579-2000

FRB Dallas
P.O. Box 655906
2200 North Pearl Street
Dallas, TX 75265-5906
214-922-6770

FRB Denver
P.O. Box 5228
1020 16th Street
Denver, CO 80217-5228
303-572-2470

FRB Detroit
P.O. Box 1059
160 West Fort Street
Detroit, MI 48231
313-964-6157

FRB El Paso
P.O. Box 100
301 East Main
El Paso, TX 79999
915-521-8272

FRB Houston
P.O. Box 2578
1701 San Jacinto Street
Houston, TX 77252
713-659-4433

FRB Jacksonville
P.O. Box 2499
800 West Water Street
Jacksonville, FL 32231-2499
904-632-1179

FRB Little Rock
P.O. Box 1261
325 West Capitol Avenue
Little Rock, AR 72203
501-324-8272

FRB Los Angeles
P.O. Box 2077
950 South Grand Avenue
Los Angeles, CA 90051
213-624-7398

FRB Louisville
P.O. Box 710
410 South Fifth Street
Louisville, KY 40232
502-568-9236

FRB Memphis
P.O. Box 407
200 North Main Street
Memphis, TN 38101
901-523-7171 Ext. 423

FRB Miami
P.O. Box 520847
9100 NW Thirty-Six Street
Miami, FL 33152
305-471-6497

FRB Minneapolis
250 Marquette Avenue
Minneapolis, MN 55480
612-340-2075

FRB Nashville
301 Eighth Avenue, North
Nashville, TN 37203-4407
615-251-7100

FRB New Orleans
P.O. Box 61630
525 St. Charles Avenue
New Orleans, LA 70161
504-593-3200

FRB New York
Federal Reserve P.O. Station
33 Liberty Street
New York, NY 100045
212-720-6619

FIGURE 10.1, Continued. Federal Reserve Banks and Branches

FRB Oklahoma City
P.O. Box 25129
226 Dean A McGee Avenue
Oklahoma City, OK 73125
405-270-8652

FRB Omaha
2201 Farnam Street
Omaha, NE 68102
402-221-5636

FRB Philadelphia
P.O. Box 90
Ten Independence Mall
Philadelphia, PA 19105
215-574-6680

FRB Pittsburgh
P.O. Box 867
717 Grant Street
Pittsburgh, PA 15230-0867
412-261-7802

FRB Portland
P.O. Box 3436
915 S.W. Stark Street
Portland, OR 97208-3436
503-221-5932

FRB Richmond
P.O. Box 27622
701 East Byrd Street
Richmond, VA 23261
804-697-8372

FRB Salt Lake City
P.O. Box 30780
120 South State Street
Salt Lake City, UT 84130-0780
801-322-7882

FRB San Antonio
P.O. Box 1471
126 East Nueva Street
San Antonio, TX 78295
512-978-1303

FRB San Francisco
P.O. Box 7702
101 Market Street
San Francisco, CA 94120
415-974-2330

FRB Seattle
P.O. Box 3567
1015 Second Avenue
Seattle, WA 98124
206-343-3605

FRB St. Louis
P.O. Box 14915
411 Locust Street
St. Louis, MO 63178
314-444-8703

Bureau of the Public Debt
Division of Customer Services
1300 C Street, S.W.
Washington, DC 20239-0001
202-874-4000

Getting Your Bond'$ Worth!

You can invest directly in U.S. Treasury securities without paying any commissions, fees, or other charges by setting up a Treasury Direct Account. This account will link up with your own bank checking or savings account. Forms you need to set up an account may be obtained by mail or in person at any Federal Reserve Bank or Branch.

11

☆ ☆ ☆ ☆ ☆ ☆ ☆ ☆ ☆ ☆ ☆ ☆ ☆ ☆ ☆ ☆ ☆

Why Mutual Funds Are a Smart Way To Buy Bonds

☆ ☆ ☆ ☆ ☆ ☆ ☆ ☆ ☆ ☆ ☆ ☆ ☆ ☆ ☆ ☆ ☆

Identifying and managing appropriate individual bonds for investment is a time-consuming process and requires a fairly high level of expertise. Because of this, many investors have found that a smart way to buy bonds is through the convenience of bond mutual funds, available through investment brokers, banks and often directly from fund companies. This approach typically results in a *higher total return* on your investment with *less risk*.

Investors are attracted to bond mutual funds for two primary reasons. The first is income: bond funds generally provide higher and steadier income than cash reserve investments such as money market funds or bank passbook accounts. Unlike stable cash reserves, however, bond funds will fluctuate in value as interest rates change. The second reason investors like bond funds is diversification: bond funds have investment characteristics that are quite different from stock funds. Though sometimes volatile, bond funds are usually considered less risky than stock funds and can serve to balance a portfolio heavy in stock funds.

A bond mutual fund is a professionally managed portfolio consisting of a group of fixed-income securities, with the primary objective of providing high current income. By combining the assets of many individual and institutional investors, the fund undertakes to invest and manage those assets more effectively than investors could do on their own.

The ability of a bond mutual fund to accomplish its goal success-fully depends first on how well it can invest a large amount of money into a portfolio of fixed-income securities that will meet its investment objective. In pursuing its goal, the fund manager evaluates the portfolio and the markets daily and decides which bonds to purchase, to hold and to sell. Plus, the fund must control its costs efficiently and provide the many services that mutual fund shareholders have come to expect.

Like other mutual funds, bond mutual funds issue their own shares and stand ready to sell new shares and redeem outstanding shares on a continuous (open-end) basis. Each share represents the same propor-tionate interest in the account (portfolio of securities) as every other share. After deduction of necessary expenses, income from the account is distributed to shareholders in the form of dividends. Invest-ment profits and losses are reflected in the value of the shares. Real-ized profits are distributed to shareholders in the form of capital gains distributions.

Benefits of Investing in Bond Mutual Funds

Diversification—bond mutual funds allow investors to spread their principal across a large number of securities, thereby cushioning the effect that one bond can have on overall investment results. As market and economic conditions change, the fund's managers can make adjustments in an attempt to meet the fund's stated objectives.

Active management—professional portfolio managers closely monitor a mutual fund, buying and selling securities when necessary. This takes the burden off investors who may not have the time to do in-depth research about various investment options. Over time, a well-run fund can give you a higher total return (income plus capital appre-ciation) than you might get by simply buying and holding individual bonds to maturity.

Cost—bond mutual funds can be bought with an initial investment that can be as low as $100, and additional investments as low as 25 dollars. Individual bonds usually require a minimum investment of $1,000 and often more, depending on the type of bond. Plus, many bond funds can be bought without paying any fee or sales commis-sion. These "no-load" funds are available directly from the fund com-panies and from certain securities brokers.

Monthly income—if you are seeking a steady stream of income, you will likely be pleased with the monthly dividends paid by most bond funds. In contrast, most individual bonds pay interest semi-annually. Of course, interest payments from an individual bond are fixed, whereas monthly dividends from a mutual fund will fluctuate with market conditions.

Liquidity—mutual funds permit you to redeem your shares at any time at the then-current market value. But remember, the market value may be more or less than your purchase cost.

No maturity date—the problem of individual bonds eventually maturing, leaving you with the lump sum that must then be reinvested (possibly at a lower interest rate) is avoided. Bond funds never mature; fund managers continually roll the proceeds from maturing securities into new bonds.

Other benefits offered by mutual funds include:

- account statements that provide a complete record of your investment activities;
- automatic reinvestment of income and capital gains distributions into additional shares of the fund;
- exchange privileges that give shareholders the right to exchange the shares owned in one fund for the shares of another fund that is part of the same group; and
- checkwriting privileges are offered by some funds that permit you to write checks against your bond fund shares. Most funds that offer this service limit the amount of each check written to at least $500.

Investment Returns on Bond Funds

With an investment in a bond mutual fund, your return comes in two forms: income return (yield) and capital return. Together they form your "total return." A bond fund's income return is its interest income expressed as a percentage of its purchase price. For instance, if you invest $10,000 in a bond fund and it pays you $800 a year, it provides an 8 percent yield. Capital return is a measure of the increase or decrease in a bond fund's market price. For instance, if your $10,000 bond fund investment drops in price to $9,700, your capital return would be -3 percent. Total return is the sum of income return plus capital return. Thus, an 8 percent yield less a 3 percent decline in principal results in a 5 percent total return.

The *income return* on a bond fund is based primarily on two factors: credit quality and maturity of bonds in the portfolio. Generally, you will earn higher yields from lower-quality bonds. Government bonds, which carry the highest credit ratings and therefore the lowest risk of default, offer the lowest yields. Investment-grade corporate bonds (rated Baa and above) provide somewhat higher yields. Non-investment grade bonds, often called "high yield" or "junk" bonds (rated Ba and below), produce the highest levels of income, but have the greatest potential for default. See Chapter 8 for more on bond credit ratings.

The maturity of a bond is set by its issuer and is expressed in days or years. For funds that hold bonds of similar credit quality, a bond fund holding longer maturity bonds will generally pay a higher yield. For instance, if a fund were to hold only 30-year Baa corporate bonds, it would typically provide a higher yield than a fund that held only three-year Baa corporate bonds.

Capital return, the gain or loss you experience as a result of changes in a bond fund's price, is mainly determined by changes in interest rates. In general, the price of a bond fund moves inversely with interest rates. When interest rates go up, bond fund prices go down, and when rates go down, bond fund prices go up. The average maturity of bonds held in a portfolio also affects capital return. In response to interest rate changes, funds that hold longer-maturity bonds will have greater price volatility than funds that hold bonds with shorter maturities.

Getting Your Bond'$ Worth!

You are likely to achieve a higher total return on your fixed-income investments, with less risk, by purchasing mutual funds. This investment choice gives you the advantages of diversification, professional management, low cost, monthly income, and liquidity. Plus, you are not faced with the problem of reinvesting the proceeds of individual bonds as they mature.

12

☆ ☆ ☆ ☆ ☆ ☆ ☆ ☆ ☆ ☆ ☆ ☆ ☆ ☆ ☆ ☆ ☆

How To Choose
a Bond Fund

☆ ☆ ☆ ☆ ☆ ☆ ☆ ☆ ☆ ☆ ☆ ☆ ☆ ☆ ☆ ☆ ☆

This chapter discusses the major types of bond mutual funds you will encounter, how they differ from one another, and factors you should consider in choosing a fund. You can utilize bond funds as a means of realizing immediate income from your capital (most bond funds pay income distributions monthly), or you can let your money accumulate in bond funds for possible income purposes at a later time.

How Bond Funds Are Classified

Types of Bond Funds

Bond mutual funds are divided into four principal classifications: U.S. Government and Agency funds, corporate funds, municipal funds and international funds.

U.S Government and Agency bond funds invest in securities that are issued by the U.S. Treasury and other governmental agencies and instrumentalities. These funds offer a higher degree of credit safety since the securities they hold are backed by the full faith and credit of the U.S. government. But remember, the market value of the funds' portfolios of securities and the funds' shares are not insured or guaranteed by the U.S. government.

The U.S. Treasury issues three types of instruments: Treasury bills (T-bills), with maturities from 90 days to one year; U.S. Treasury notes (T-notes), with maturities from one to ten years; and U.S. Treasury bonds (T-bonds), with maturities from ten to 30 years. Other such governmental bonds include certificates issued by the Government National Mortgage Association (GNMA or Ginnie Mae). GNMA securities are explicitly guaranteed by the U.S. government, while other government agency securities carry a less formal backing.

Corporate bond funds hold debt obligations issued by corporations in various maturities and yields. Since these bonds are not guaranteed as to the timely payment of interest and principal, mutual fund portfolio managers look at their credit ratings, if any, to assess their relative risk.

Municipal bond funds invest in bonds issued by states and local governments to finance schools, highways, airports, bridges, hospitals, water and sewer works, and other public projects. In most cases, income earned from these securities is exempt from federal income taxes and, in some instances, state and local taxes as well in an investor's state of residence. Like corporate bonds, municipals are carefully assessed by portfolio managers to evaluate their level of credit risk.

International bond funds, sometimes called "World" or "Global" bond funds, invest in the debt securities of companies and countries throughout the world, and may include the United States. Portfolio managers investing in foreign bonds must take into account international currency fluctuations as well as possible credit risk of the securities they buy.

Maturity Classifications

In addition to being categorized by issuer, bond mutual funds can be classified according to the average maturity of the portfolio, as follows:

Short-term bond funds typically have average maturities ranging between one and five years. Such funds normally pay lower yields, but offer greater price stability than comparable longer-term funds.

Intermediate-term bond funds usually have average maturities ranging between three and ten years. These funds should offer higher yields than more stable, shorter-term bond funds and offer greater price stability than longer-term, higher-yielding bond funds.

Long-term bond funds generally have average maturities greater than ten years. These funds typically pay the highest yields, but they are also usually the most volatile.

Factors To Consider in Selecting a Bond Fund

When choosing a bond fund for investment, there are five factors you should consider.

1. *Are you investing for current income or for future growth?* If your objective is to receive income, remember that even as bond prices fall in reaction to a rise in interest rates, they may be offset by higher yields to help you earn the income you need. Look for funds that may provide the level of income you need at the level or risk appropriate for you. If you reinvest your dividends, think of your fund as a growth investment, and seek funds that have the potential to provide competitive total returns over the long term.

2. *What is the time frame of your investment?* If you are thinking in terms of one year or less, you may want to consider a money market fund rather than a bond fund. With a money market fund you will receive a yield that is competitive with short-term securities and you won't have to worry about any fluctuation in the value of your principal. Beyond that, the longer the average maturity of a fund's holdings, the greater the volatility of the fund. A fund with a longer average maturity may fluctuate too much for investors with short time horizons, while one with a shorter average maturity may not yield enough to produce sufficient returns for investors with long time frames.

3. *How do you feel about the potential risks of your investment?* Although your decision about which type of fund is most appropriate should be based primarily on your goals and time horizon, your tolerance for risk should also be considered. You can choose among a variety of bond funds, such as government funds (conservative), investment-grade corporate funds (moderate risk), and junk bond funds (aggressive), among others.

4. *How has a fund you are considering performed in the past?* While past performance is not a guarantee of future results, you can get an idea of how a bond fund may perform in the future by looking at its past returns. But be sure to look at performance based on your needs. If you're investing for total return (yield plus capital change), review the average annual total return over the long term. If you're investing for current income, look at the payment amounts (dividend rate). And if you are concerned with volatility, check how much the price has fluctuated during periods of various market conditions. See the appendix for services that provide fund rankings and information.

5. *Consider a fund's operating expenses and possible sales charges.* All mutual funds have operating expenses that include the costs of managing a fund. These expenses are paid from the earnings of the fund before they are distributed and are not charged directly to your shareholder account. Expenses are typically higher for funds that involve more credit risk because extra resources are needed to monitor such funds' holdings. For instance, according to Lipper Analytical Services, the average expense ratio (the total of expenses and fees divided by the fund's average assets) for Treasury bond funds is 0.73 percent. For non-investment-grade bond funds, the average is 1.24 percent. Generally, the lower the operating expenses are for comparable funds, the higher will be your return.

Some bond funds have sales charges, or loads, that are deducted from the amount of your initial investment, and some funds also charge a redemption fee for shares sold within a certain period. Other things being equal, your investment return will be better from funds that levy no purchase or redemption fees.

Getting Your Bond'$ Worth!

You can utilize bond funds as a means of realizing immediate income from your capital (most bond funds pay income distributions monthly), or you can let your money accumulate in bond funds for possible income purposes at a later time. When choosing a bond fund, consider such factors as your goals, your time frame, your tolerance for risk, and the fund's past performance. Other things being equal, your investment return will be better if you avoid funds that levy purchase or redemption fees.

13

☆ ☆ ☆ ☆ ☆ ☆ ☆ ☆ ☆ ☆ ☆ ☆ ☆ ☆ ☆

Minimizing the Cost of Investing in Bond Funds

☆ ☆ ☆ ☆ ☆ ☆ ☆ ☆ ☆ ☆ ☆ ☆ ☆ ☆ ☆

It will cost you money to invest in mutual funds. As an investor, however, you have a great deal of control over how much that cost will be. One of the wonders of mutual funds is their cost efficiency. The economies of scale enjoyed by large investment companies are passed on to the individual investor in the form of low expenses, which translates into higher investment returns (assuming able management). In addition, a great opportunity available to investors today is the ability to buy into some of the best professionally managed portfolios of bonds (and stocks) without a broker and without paying any sales commissions. This is easily done by investing in *no-load funds*. These funds sell their shares directly to the public, and in most cases, with no sales charges, thus avoiding fees and commissions not relevant to investment performance.

No-Load Funds

The first mutual funds to be sold without commission were offered in the early 1920s. Now more than 1,000 no-load mutual funds are priced daily in the mutual fund sections of *The New York Times, The Wall Street Journal, Barron's,* and other major newspapers. They can be purchased on a direct basis and at no cost to the investor. Of course, there are certain operating expenses and management fees that are common to all mutual funds.

More and more investors are buying mutual funds directly from fund companies and avoiding payment of any sales fees or commissions. Unlike opening an account at a bank, mutual fund investors can open an account and make investments without ever setting foot into their offices. This is done by dealing with no-load mutual fund companies. No-load funds are exactly like load funds in every respect except that shares of no-load funds are purchased directly from the fund company and without the addition of a sales commission.

Today, the distinction between no-load and load funds has become somewhat blurred. Some funds marketed as no-load do, in fact, levy certain charges that are not related to the cost of investment management. These charges may include annual sales distribution fees (rule 12b-1) adopted by the Securities and Exchange Commission under the Investment Company Act of 1940. Such fees can have an adverse impact on a fund's performance, especially when compared with similar funds that do not charge 12b-1 fees. The mutual fund listings in major daily newspapers indicate which funds charge these fees.

Other charges made by some funds include low loads, back-end loads, contingent deferred sales charges, and fixed redemption charges or exit fees. A recent study by *Morningstar, Inc.* in Chicago, Illinois, found that 28 percent of all mutual funds are pure no-load, 8 percent are no-loads with 12b-1 fees, 10 percent have back-end loads and 12b-1 fees, 34 percent are front-end loads plus 12b-1 fees, and 20 percent are front-end load only.

Load Funds

A sales commission, or *load,* charged by many mutual funds, does not compensate the funds' investment managers. Fund managers are compensated through a management fee that is charged against the fund. All funds, load and no-load, have management fees. In the case of a load fund, the sales charge is made in addition to the annual management fee, which generally runs between 0.5 and 1 percent of the fund's assets. Independent studies have consistently shown there is no difference in performance, on average, between the two types when the load is disregarded.

The maximum permitted sales charge (load) is 8.5 percent. However, since an 8.5 percent load is stated as a percentage of the total purchase price (net asset value divided by the sales charge), the ratio of the load to the net amount invested in the fund is actually 9.3 percent. For example, if you purchase shares of a load fund for $10,000, $850 goes to the sales organization; the balance, $9,150, is actually invested in the fund and is the net asset value of the shares purchased. The $850 lost to you represents 9.3 percent of the value of the shares you have bought ($850 divided by $9,150).

In recent years many load funds have reduced sales charges to the 3-5 percent range, with the difference being made up through so-called back-end loads, contingent deferred sales charges and/or 12b-1 fees. From an investment performance standpoint, the effect of a load is felt throughout the term of a shareholder's investment. This is because less money has been at work than would have been the case if the full amount of the purchase price were invested in a no-load fund.

The difference in growth of an investment of $10,000 in two comparable funds—one with an 8.5 percent load, the other no-load—can be dramatic. Over ten years, with an assumed 10 percent rate of return, the no-load fund earns $2,204 more. Figure 13.1 illustrates how this works.

The load fund investor was $850 behind at the beginning (8.5 percent of $10,000) and forever loses the 10 percent growth on that portion of the investment. Over an investing lifetime, the difference becomes greatly magnified.

FIGURE 13.1 $10,000 Invested at an Assumed Rate of 10 Percent

	Net Amount Invested	Value in Ten Years
Load Fund	$ 9,150	$23,735
No-Load Fund	10,000	25,939

Explanation of Other Marketing Charges

The other charges made by mutual fund companies include contingent sales charges, exit fees, 12b-1 distribution fees and dividend reinvestment fees.

- *Contingent sales charges* (often called *back-end loads*) are paid to selling organizations and salespeople and can be as much as 5-6 percent for shareholders redeeming shares in the first year, declining by 1 percent per year for the next 5 to 6 years.
- *Exit fees* are the small administrative charges some management companies make either to withdraw or switch from one fund under its management to another such fund.
- *12b-1 distribution fees* permit a fund's management to use fund assets to pay for distribution costs, including advertising, distribution of fund literature such as prospectuses and annual reports, and sales commissions paid to brokers who distribute the fund. The 12b-1 fees range from as low as 0.25 percent to as much as 1.00 percent per year and are deducted from a fund's assets.
- *Dividend reinvestment fees* are charges imposed by a few fund managers for reinvesting the shareholder's dividend distributions.

Look For Mutual Funds with Low Operating Expenses

All mutual fund companies are in business to make a profit. The cost to an investor of owning mutual fund shares can range from as little as 0.18 percent to as much as 2 percent or more. These costs are in the form of the fund's expense ratio (including investment advisory fees, distribution charges and other operating expenses) and portfolio transaction costs (brokerage and other trading costs), which are deducted from the assets managed by the fund. The average general equity fund has an annual expense ratio of 1.3 percent of investor assets. Portfolio transaction costs typically run between 0.5 percent to 1 percent. Funds with a low expense ratio and low transaction costs can have an important positive impact on the returns you receive as an investor.

The manager of a mutual fund has, in effect, one client with one investment objective and a single set of investment policies. The larger the fund, the more cost-effective it may become. While big funds often require more personnel to run them than do small funds, the number of people needed becomes proportionately much smaller as the size of the fund grows. The Franklin U.S. Government Securities Fund, for example, with $11 billion in assets in early 1995, charges a management fee of 0.45 percent of average net assets. With other expenses of 0.13 percent, total fund operating expenses run to 0.58 percent of assets. This one fund provides annual revenue of more than $63 million to the Franklin group of funds. While providing a large source of income for Franklin, the 0.58 percent cost to the investor is quite modest.

Other funds charge more or less, depending largely on the efficiency of their operations. Small funds, or those just getting started, will of necessity run higher total operating costs than their larger peers. For example, the Eaton Vance Marathon High Income Fund, with over $425 million in assets in late 1994, had total operating costs that were 1.82 percent of assets. At the low end is the Vanguard Bond Index Fund–Total Bond Market Portfolio. Its total operating expenses have been running at 0.18 percent of the $2 billion it has under management.

The management fee is usually the largest part of total expenses. It covers the salaries of fund officers and other employees as well as expenses relating to office space and facilities, and the payment for investment management and advice. Other operating expenses borne by the fund include charges of the fund's custodian (the bank or other financial institution that keeps custody of stock and bond certificates and other assets of the fund), accountants and attorneys, the cost of issuing share certificates and disbursing dividends, and expenses for printing, postage and mailing.

Expenses are paid by a fund primarily out of investment income, which is more than sufficient in most cases. An exception would be funds that invest substantially in the common stock of growth companies that pay few or no dividends. When investment income is not sufficient to cover expenses, the balance is paid out of invested capital.

Every mutual fund must report its expense charges annually in its prospectus, so investors can easily compare charges from one fund to another. Expense charges are just one factor to consider in the selection of a fund; other things being equal (management ability, past performance, investment objectives and policies), a fund with low expenses will tend to produce a better return for the investor than will one with charges that are out of line with the competition.

Getting Your Bond'$ Worth!

Today you can buy into some of the best professionally managed portfolios of bonds (and stocks) without a broker and without paying any sales commissions by investing in no-load funds. Other charges to watch out for include low loads, back-end loads, contingent deferred sales charges, and fixed redemption charges or exit fees. Look for funds with a low expense ratio and low transaction costs; they can have an important impact on your investment returns.

14

☆ ☆ ☆ ☆ ☆ ☆ ☆ ☆ ☆ ☆ ☆ ☆ ☆ ☆ ☆ ☆ ☆

How a Prospectus Can Help You

☆ ☆ ☆ ☆ ☆ ☆ ☆ ☆ ☆ ☆ ☆ ☆ ☆ ☆ ☆ ☆ ☆

The most important source of information available to mutual fund investors is the *prospectus*. The law stipulates that the offering of any mutual fund for sale to the public must be accompanied or preceded by a prospectus.

A prospectus sets forth the information that a prospective investor should know about a specific mutual fund before investing. For more detailed information, a *statement of additional information* may be obtained without charge by writing or calling the mutual fund company. The statement, which is incorporated by reference into the prospectus, has been filed with the Securities and Exchange Commission (SEC). Each prospectus also is required to display prominently the following statement: "These securities have not been approved or disapproved by the Securities and Exchange Commission or any state securities commission, nor has the Securities and Exchange Commission or any state securities commission passed upon the accuracy of adequacy of this prospectus. Any representation to the contrary is a criminal offense."

Before permitting a mutual fund company to offer a fund for sale to the public, the SEC examines the statement to be sure that it contains all the information that is required by law. When that requirement has been met, the fund company is notified that it may offer its fund for sale to the public.

What the Prospectus Contains: The Strong Government Securities Fund

For illustration purposes, let's take a look at some of the information contained in the May, 1994, prospectus of the Strong Government Securities Fund. You will find this same type of data in the prospectuses of most mutual funds.

Investment Objectives and Policies

Page I-22 of the Strong Government Securities Fund's 1994 prospectus sets forth in typical fashion the information investors want to know about the investment objectives and policies of the Fund. It states that the Fund's *investment objective* is "to obtain a high level of current income from investments principally in a diversified portfolio of U.S. government securities." The Fund is designed primarily for investors who seek higher yields than money market funds offer and the low credit risk that U.S. government securities carry but who are willing to accept some principal fluctuation in order to achieve that objective.

The Fund's investment policy—how it intends to accomplish its objective—is to invest "at least 80 percent of its assets in U.S. government securities under normal market conditions." The prospectus defines "U.S. government securities" as securities issued or guaranteed by the U.S. government or its agencies or instrumentalities. Investments may include securities such as: U.S. Treasury bills, notes, and bonds; obligations of the Federal Housing Administration, Farmers Home Administration, Export-Import Bank of the United States, Small Business Administration; and the Government National Mortgage Association (including GNMA pass-through certificates), whose securities are supported by the full faith and credit of the United States; among others. The balance of its net assets may be invested in other investment-grade fixed-income securities." The Fund does not invest in non-investment grade securities.

The prospectus goes on to warn that the prices of government securities and other fixed-income securities are affected by changes in the prevailing level of interest rates even though these investments offer a stable stream of income. It notes that since these securities generally experience appreciation when interest rates decline and depreciation when interest rates rise, the Fund's portfolio will react in a similar manner.

A reminder: Always review a fund's investment objective and policy. Occasionally, a fund's name can be misleading. For instance, you would not know from its name that the Templeton Income Fund invests mainly in foreign securities.

Fund Expenses

The prospectus of every mutual fund includes a table illustrating all the expenses and fees you would incur as a shareholder of the fund.

Shareholder transaction expenses include any sales load imposed on purchases and those imposed on reinvested dividends, as well as redemption fees and exchange fees. In the case of many no-load funds, there are no charges for any of these activities. Other funds indicate their charges as a percentage of net asset value or dollar amount.

The Strong Government Securities Fund prospectus lists the following schedule of expenses:

Shareholder Transaction Expenses

Sales Load Imposed on Purchases	None
Sales Load Imposed on Reinvested Dividends	None
Deferred Sales Load	None
Redemption Fees	None
Exchange Fees	None

Annual Fund Operating Expenses
(as a percentage of average net assets)

Management Fees	.60
Other Expenses	.36
12b-1 Fees	None
Total Operating Expenses	.96

Footnotes indicate that there are certain charges associated with retirement accounts and with certain services offered by the Fund. Purchases and redemption of shares can be made through broker-dealers or others who may charge a commission or other transaction fee for their services.

Selected Per-Share Data and Ratios

The Strong Government Securities Fund prospectus provides a table with financial highlights beginning on October 29, 1986, the date the Fund was established, through December 31, 1993. Figure 14.1 reproduces this information from pages I-10 and I-11 of the prospectus. It permits an investor to see the Fund's financial results for the period shown.

Other Important Information

Mutual fund prospectuses contain a host of other information that is important to potential investors. The following information is typical of what you will find in most prospectuses:

Performance Record.   Many funds include in their prospectuses the investment results for several periods throughout the fund's lifetime to help an investor see how money invested in the fund has fared in the past. A few funds provide a complete history of their investment returns. In the case of some funds, such a the Strong Government Securities Fund, historical return data may be omitted.

Opening an Account.   Each prospectus includes information on how to open an account and purchase shares in the fund, and will be accompanied by an Account Registration Form. Your purchase must be equal to or greater than the minimum initial investment. Depending on the fund, this may range from as little as $50 to more than 50,000 dollars. Most funds can be started in the $1,000–$3,000 range.

Fund shares may be purchased by mail, by wire, by exchange from another fund in the same family of funds, directly from your checking account, and through other means that are explained in the prospectus.

When opening a new mutual fund account, you must select one of three distribution options:

1. *Automatic reinvestment option.* Both dividends and capital gains distributions will be reinvested in additional shares of the fund.

FIGURE 14.1 Sample Financial Highlights—Strong Government Securities Fund

STRONG GOVERNMENT SECURITIES FUND

	1994	1993	1992	1991	1990	1989	1988	1987	1986**
Net Asset Value, Beginning of Period	$ 10.61	$ 10.39	$ 10.77	$ 10.10	$ 10.08	$ 9.98	$ 9.75	$ 10.09	$ 10.00
Income From Investment Operations									
Net Investment Income	0.62	0.66	0.80	0.77	0.72	0.78	0.68	0.65	0.13
Net Realized and Unrealized Gains (Losses) on Investments	(0.98)	0.63	0.11	0.84	0.12	0.17	0.32	(0.34)	0.09
Total from Investment Operations	(0.36)	1.29	0.91	1.61	0.84	0.95	1.00	0.31	0.22
Less Distributions									
From Net Investment Income	(0.62)	(0.66)	(0.80)	(0.77)	(0.72)	(0.78)	(0.68)	(0.65)	(0.13)
From Net Realized Gains	—	(0.32)	(0.49)	(0.17)	(0.10)	(0.07)	(0.09)	—	—
In Excess of Net Realized Gains	—	(0.09)	—	—	—	—	—	—	—
Total Distributions	(0.62)	(1.07)	(1.29)	(0.94)	(0.82)	(0.85)	(0.77)	(0.65)	(0.13)
Net Asset Value, End of Period	$ 9.63	$ 10.61	$ 10.39	$ 10.77	$ 10.10	$ 10.08	$ 9.98	$ 9.75	$ 10.09
Total Return	-3.4%	+12.7%	+9.2%	+16.7%	+8.7%	+9.9%	+10.5%	+3.4%	+2.2%
Net Assets, End of Period (In Thousands)	$ 276,832	$ 221,961	$ 82,169	$ 51,934	$ 41,099	$ 35,119	$ 25,408	$ 11,380	$ 880
Ratio of Expenses to Average Net Assets	0.9%	0.8%	0.7%	0.8%	1.3%	1.3%	0.4%	1.0%	0.6%*
Ratio of Expenses to Average Net Assets Without Waivers and Absorptions	0.9%	1.0%	1.2%	1.4%	1.5%	1.6%	1.6%	1.6%	1.2%*
Ratio of Net Investment Income to Average Net Assets	6.2%	6.0%	7.7%	7.5%	7.2%	7.6%	6.9%	6.6%	7.2%*
Portfolio Turnover Rate	479.0%	520.9%	628.8%	292.9%	254.2%	421.6%	1,727.8%	715.0%	0.0%*

*Calculated on an annualized basis.
**Inception date is October 24, 1986. Total return is not annualized.

Source: Reprinted by permission of the Strong Funds.

2. *Cash dividend option.* Your dividends will be paid in cash and capital gains will be reinvested in additional fund shares.
3. *All-cash option.* Dividend and capital gains distributions will be paid in cash.

Some funds permit distributions to be reinvested automatically in shares of another fund of the same family.

Important Tax Note: If you purchase shares shortly before a distribution of dividends or capital gains, a portion of your investment will be returned to you as a taxable distribution (regardless of whether you are reinvesting your distributions or taking them in cash). For example, suppose you purchase shares of a fund at $15.00 each and the next day the fund pays a $2.00 distribution. You will be credited with $2.00, but you will have incurred a $2.00 tax liability, while the net asset value per share will drop by $2.00.

Fund Management. This section explains who is responsible for overall management of the fund, as well as who provides the professional investment supervision. Information about the organizations and individuals providing management is given, including their background and professional credentials.

The fee structure to be paid for management services and how it is to be charged is set forth. In the case of the Strong Government Securities Fund, the investment advisor is paid a monthly advisory fee based on a percentage of the Fund's average daily net asset value. The annual rate is 0.60 percent.

Share Price Calculation. In this section, the prospectus explains how and when share prices are calculated. The price of a fund's shares on any given day is their *net asset value* (NAV). This figure is computed by dividing the total market value of a fund's investments and other assets on that day, less any liabilities, by the number of shares outstanding. The NAV of the shares of a fund is determined at 4:00 PM Eastern time on each day the New York Stock Exchange is open for trading.

Tax-Advantaged Retirement Plans. Most mutual fund companies offer tax-advantaged retirement plans to their shareholders. The following plans are among the most popular:

- *Individual retirement plan.* A plan offering individuals with earned income the opportunity to compound earnings on a tax-deferred basis.
- *Keogh plan.* A tax-advantaged plan for self-employed individuals and their employees that permits the employer to make annual tax-deductible contributions of up to $30,000.
- *Corporate retirement plans.* Retirement plans for large or small corporate entities that can help a company attract and retain valuable employees.

Purchase of Shares in the Fund. A prospectus will explain how shares may be purchased and whether you must go through a registered representative or may buy shares directly from the fund. Other information you may need to know is included, such as minimum investment requirements and methods of purchasing shares (i.e., by phone, by mail, in person, or by automatic investment).

Exchanges Between Funds. Shares can be sold by exchanging from one mutual fund to another in the same family of funds. It is important to remember that this constitutes a taxable event, and any gain or loss is reportable for income tax purposes. (Some funds charge a small fee, e.g., $5 for exchanges.)

Redeeming Shares. Mutual funds may be redeemed at the NAV per share that is next determined after receipt of proper redemption instructions. You may redeem your shares by telephone or by mail. Telephone redemption orders received prior to 4:00 PM (Eastern time) on any business day will be redeemed at the NAV determined for that day.

Automatic Reinvestment Plan. A fast, convenient way to make regular mutual fund investments to an account already established is the *automatic reinvestment plan.* Investments may be made by authorized transfers from a bank checking or savings account and by direct deposit of all or a portion of a payroll or government check. Depending on the requirements of the fund, such investments can be made twice monthly, monthly or quarterly. Minimum amounts are stipulated in the prospectus.

Miscellaneous Information. The prospectus also contains other information that you will find helpful in establishing and maintaining a mutual fund investment:

- *Signature guarantees.* For certain written transaction requests, most funds require that your signature be guaranteed by a bank, trust company or member of a domestic stock exchange. Having a document notarized does not qualify as a signature guarantee.
- *Certificates.* Most funds will issue share certificates on request.
- *Canceling trades.* A trade received by the fund in writing or by telephone, if believed to be authentic, may not normally be canceled. This would include purchases, exchanges, or redemptions.

Getting Your Bond'$ Worth!

Review your fund's prospectus before investing, and keep the most current one in your records. It is your most important source of valuable information, including investment objectives and policies, expenses and fees, historical performance data, a guide on how to open an account, and the various services furnished by the fund.

15

☆ ☆ ☆ ☆ ☆ ☆ ☆ ☆ ☆ ☆ ☆ ☆ ☆ ☆ ☆ ☆ ☆ ☆

One-Stop Bond Fund Shopping

☆ ☆ ☆ ☆ ☆ ☆ ☆ ☆ ☆ ☆ ☆ ☆ ☆ ☆ ☆ ☆ ☆ ☆

Fund shopping networks are among the newest services available to mutual fund investors through discount brokers. These networks enable you to buy and sell a wide range of no-load, low-load, and load mutual funds through one source. When you invest through one of these one-stop sources, you can choose from more than 2,400 stock and bond mutual funds sponsored by more than 125 leading companies. And the number continues to grow. According to Don Phillips, vice president of Morningstar, Inc., the networks will become the dominant way to distribute mutual funds.

The basic idea is simple: You can buy and sell shares in numerous no-load funds without paying a transaction fee. That means you're putting the full value of your dollars to work for your investments. Transaction fees are charged on certain no-load funds, generally those that have chosen not to participate in the program. Load funds can also be purchased in some programs, in which case you will be charged the sales load as described in the prospectus. Business can be transacted with one telephone call, and everything is clearly summarized on one statement.

The two biggest programs in terms of assets are Charles Schwab's *Mutual Fund OneSource,* with more than $10 billion under management, and Fidelity Investment's *FundsNetwork,* with $5 billion. Other companies offering similar plans include Jack White & Company, Muriel Siebert & Company, and Waterhouse Securities.

How One-Stop Shopping Plans Work for You

You pay no loads or transactions fees to invest in a wide range of no-load funds available from different fund companies. The price you pay is the same as investing directly with the fund itself.

Whatever your investment objective, from capital preservation to aggressive growth, a one-source mutual fund service gives you a nearly complete range of funds to choose from to help you reach your objective. You can move easily between funds, even if they're from different fund companies. This way you can adjust your mutual fund portfolio to reflect changing investment goals or market conditions.

Once you have established an account, you can invest in hundreds of mutual funds with a single phone call. Some firms offer limited commission-free trading and will buy funds on margin or sell short, two highly speculative trading techniques.

Because fund companies pay to participate, organizations that offer no-transaction-fee mutual fund network services are compensated by fees received directly from the fund companies. These fees range from 0.20 percent to 0.35 percent of the assets managed by the program. As long as these costs are not passed along to shareholders and fund expense ratios stay at reasonable levels, this should not be a problem to investors.

Although the general approaches for companies providing one-stop shopping plans are straightforward and pretty much the same, there are some differences. To get started, you must first open a discount brokerage account with the firm of your choice. This gives you access to the mutual fund network plus the opportunity to trade in stocks, bonds and other securities. Then, to purchase shares, instruct your representative the name of the fund, the dollar amount you want to invest and whether you want fund dividends and capital gains paid in cash or automatically reinvested in more fund shares. To sell, you need only to name the fund, the number of shares you wish to sell,and whether you want to receive the proceeds or have them credited to your account.

The fund consolidators maintain single, multimillion-dollar accounts at the mutual fund families, so they have some flexibility on minimum investment requirements. Schwab's OneSource program, for instance, has minimums that range from $250 to $2,000, which in some cases is below what you would have to invest when dealing directly with a fund.

One problem with the one-stop shopping system is that several excellent fund families, including T. Rowe Price, Scudder, USAA, and Vanguard, do not participate in any of the "free" programs. However, they are available if a transaction fee is paid. Generally, firms offering the program will let you transfer most outside funds into your consolidated account, at no extra cost. This way you can easily keep track of your holdings.

The Major Players

To give you a general means of comparison, following are the major players in the game and a summary of their current rules for their one-stop mutual fund shopping programs. Prices and rules can change, so contact the broker.

Fidelity Investments
161 Devonshire Street
Boston, MA 02110
800-544-9697

Service: *FundsNetwork*

Buying or Selling. Fidelity equity fund purchases, both load and no-load, in FundsNetwork must be paid for within five business days of purchase. Fidelity *bond* funds must be paid for the following business day. Most other no-load funds purchased through FundsNetwork must be paid for the next business day. Other load funds must be paid for within five business days.

No transaction fees apply to purchases, sales, or exchanges of the participating no-load funds offered through FundsNetwork. Fidelity provides a directory of participating funds. Fees for non-participating no-load funds are determined by transaction amount and apply to both purchases and redemptions. A minimum fee of $28 applies to all transactions other than Fidelity funds. Fees start at $17.50 plus 0.8 percent of the principal amount for transactions of $5,000 or less, and decline to $157.50 plus 0.08 percent for transactions in excess of 95,000 dollars. If you purchase a no-load fund and pay a transaction fee, you must pay a transaction fee upon its sale. For load funds, you are charged the sales load as described in the prospectus.

Moving Money Between Funds.   You pay no charge for moving money between participating funds in *FundsNetwork*. If you move money between funds that do not participate in *FundsNetwork,* you'll pay the standard fee to buy or sell, with a $28 minimum.

Pricing Cut-Off Times.   Buy and sell orders for Fidelity funds (except for Fidelity Select funds, where hourly pricing applies) placed by 4:00 PM Eastern time (1:00 PM Pacific time) are executed at that day's price. Orders placed after the cut-off time are executed at the next day's price. Orders for other no-load funds, including participating funds, have a cut-off time of 1:00 PM Eastern time. The cut-off time for load funds is 4:00 PM Eastern time. Exchanges within the same fund family have a cut-off time of 2:30 PM Eastern time.

Trading Frequency.   Fidelity reserves the right to charge transaction fees if you make five or more short-term redemptions (shares held less than six months) on funds available without transaction fees through *FundsNetwork* in a 12-month period.

Charles Schwab & Co., Inc.
101 Montgomery Street
San Francisco, CA 94104
800-526-8600

Service: *Mutual Fund OneSource*

Buying or Selling.   When buying, you must have sufficient cash in your Schwab account to cover your purchase, plus any applicable transaction fees. You pay no fee to buy or sell *Mutual Fund One-Source* funds (funds that participate in Schwab's program) or *Schwab-Funds* (the registered name for Schwab's own mutual funds). To buy or sell other funds, you will pay a transaction fee (minimum $29 per trade) according to Schwab's schedule. The fees decline from 0.6 percent of principal on transactions of $15,000 or less to 0.08 percent on transactions in excess of 100,000 dollars.

Moving Money Between Funds.   You pay no charge for moving money between *Mutual Fund OneSource* funds or *SchwabFunds*. With non-participating funds you will pay the standard fee on the sell order ($29 per trade minimum) and a $15 fee on the buy order.

Pricing Cut-Off Times. Buy and sell orders for most equity mutual funds (except for *SchwabFunds*) placed by 2:00 PM Eastern time (11:00 AM Pacific time) are executed at that day's price. Orders placed after 2:00 PM are executed at the next day's price. Orders for *SchwabFunds* have a cut-off time of 4:00 PM. Buy orders for most bond funds have a cut-off time of 9:00 PM Eastern time and are priced at the next day's close. Orders cannot be changed or canceled after the cut-off time.

Trading Frequency. If you make five or more short-term redemptions of *Mutual Fund OneSource* funds over any 12-month period, Schwab will start charging you transaction fees on all your mutual fund trades. A short-term redemption refers to the sale of mutual fund shares held for six months or less. Redemptions in Schwab's own funds and funds that charge a load of 4 percent or more with which Schwab has formal distribution agreements are not included.

Muriel Siebert & Co., Inc.
885 Third Avenue
New York, NY 10022-4834
800-872-0666

Service: *FundExchange*

Buying or Selling. You pay no fee to buy or sell *FundExchange* funds (funds that participate in the Muriel Siebert & Co. program). To buy or sell other funds, you pay a transaction fee (minimum $39.50 per trade) according to Siebert's fee schedule. The fees decline from $17.50 plus 0.8 percent of principal on transactions of $5,000 or less to $157.50 plus 0.08 percent on transactions in excess of 100,000 dollars.

Redemptions. No transaction fee will be charged on any redemption of shares originally purchased through Muriel Siebert's No Transaction Fee Program *and* held beyond the short-term holding period. The duration of the short-term holding period varies with the amount invested per fund as follows: $2,000 to $9,999 = 9 months; $10,000 to $19,999 = 6 months; $10,000 to $49,999 = 3 months; and $50,000 and over = 1 month. If shares are redeemed before the short-term holding period has elapsed, the firm's standard commission schedule for no-load mutual funds will apply to the sale only.

Waterhouse Securities, Inc.
100 Wall Street
New York, NY 10005
800-934-4443

Service: *Mutual FundConnection*

Buying or Selling.   When buying, you must have sufficient cash in your account for settlement before a transaction can be executed. Credit balances in your account can be invested in one of three money market funds available at Waterhouse.

No transaction fees apply to purchases, sales, or exchanges of the participating no-load funds offered through *FundConnection*. Waterhouse provides a directory of participating funds. Fees for other no-load funds are determined by transaction amount and apply to both purchases and redemptions. A minimum fee of $29 applies to all transactions. Fees start at 0.6 percent of the principal amount for transactions of $15,000 or less and decline to 0.08 percent for transactions in excess of 100,000 dollars. When buying load funds, you are charged the sales load as described in the prospectus. Sell orders for load funds will be executed for a flat $35 transaction fee.

Moving Money Between Funds.   If you simultaneously switch from one mutual fund to another, Waterhouse will charge a transaction fee on the sale, but execute the buy order for only $15. These charges do not apply to those no-load funds that do not have a transaction fee.

Pricing Cut-Off Times.   Buy and sell orders must be entered by 2:00 PM Eastern time to be executed at the closing price for your fund on the day you place your order. However, most bond funds will be executed the following day.

Trading Frequency.   Waterhouse will reinstate transaction fees on an account if five or more short-term redemptions (shares held less than six months) are executed within a 12-month period.

Jack White & Company
9191 Towne Centre Drive
San Diego, CA 92122
800-323-3263

Service: *Mutual Fund Network*

Buying or Selling.   No transaction fees apply to purchases, sales, or exchanges of the mutual funds participating in Jack White & Company's No Transaction Fee Mutual Fund program. The minimum initial transaction and any subsequent transactions must total at least 5,000 dollars; otherwise, a fee of $27 is charged. Transactions in a participating fund require a 60-day holding period to avoid any transaction charges. Any positions liquidated within 60 days of purchase will be charged scheduled fees for the sale. More than 350 funds participate in the program; additional funds are added regularly.

The firm also offers more than 2,400 mutual funds, including more than 900 no-load and low-load mutual funds at low transaction fees in its *Mutual Fund Network*. Fees start at $27 for transactions in an amount up to 5,000 dollars. For transactions of $5,001 to $25,000, the fee is $35, and for transactions in excess of $25,000 the fee is 50 dollars. For load funds, you are charged the sales load as described in the prospectus.

Shorting of Mutual Funds.   Subject to availability, you can sell short shares of selected mutual funds. Because the firm maintains an extensive inventory of some of the most popularly held funds, it can take your orders to sell short, just as you would a stock. Transaction fees are the same as stated above.

Pricing Cut-Off Times.   All cut-off times are Pacific time. Phone or letter redemptions will be executed the same day if received by 12:00 PM (except for certain funds, as specified in company instructions).

Getting Your Bond'$ Worth!

You can buy and sell a wide range of no-load, low-load, and load mutual funds sponsored by more than 125 leading companies through one source, without paying any sales commissions or transaction fees. One-stop mutual fund shopping networks allow you to choose from more than 2,400 mutual funds. And you can move easily between funds, even if they are from different fund companies, thereby adjusting your mutual fund portfolio to reflect changing investment goals or market conditions.

16

☆ ☆ ☆ ☆ ☆ ☆ ☆ ☆ ☆ ☆ ☆ ☆ ☆ ☆ ☆ ☆ ☆ ☆

Discovering How Bond Funds Can Give You Your Money'$ Worth!

☆ ☆ ☆ ☆ ☆ ☆ ☆ ☆ ☆ ☆ ☆ ☆ ☆ ☆ ☆ ☆ ☆ ☆

Whether your needs are short- or long-term, you will find that there are many types of fixed-income mutual funds, with their own unique set of characteristics. These funds pool together the investment capital of people who share the same investment goals and the goals of each fund are outlined in its prospectus. Fund managers continuously buy and sell securities in an effort to build a strong portfolio and increase the overall returns for investors. Unlike individual bonds, a mutual fund does not have a maturity date. Income earned on investments is paid to the fund and generally distributed in monthly or quarterly dividends to shareholders.

Bond funds are subject to four types of risk that are inherent in fixed-income securities:

1. *Interest rate risk* is the potential for fluctuations in bond prices due to changing interest rates. In general, bond prices vary inversely with interest rates. When interest rates *rise,* bond prices generally *fall.* Conversely, when interest rates *fall,* bond prices generally *rise.* The change in price depends on a number of factors, including the bond's maturity date. Usually, bonds with longer maturities are more sensitive to changes in interest rates than bonds with shorter maturities.

2. *Income risk* is the potential for a decline in a fund's income due to falling market interest rates.

3. *Credit risk* is the possibility that a bond issuer will fail to make timely payments of either interest or principal to a fund.

4. *Prepayment risk* (for mortgage-backed securities) or *call risk* (for corporate bonds) is the likelihood that, during periods of falling interest rates, securities with high stated interest rates will be prepaid (or "called") prior to maturity, requiring a fund to invest the proceeds at generally lower interest rates.

Figure 16.1 summarizes interest rate, credit, income and prepayment/call risks for each of eight types of bond funds with various maturities. As shown, interest rate risk should be low for short-term funds, moderate for intermediate-term funds, and high for long-term funds.

As an investor, it is important for you to consider the possible risks and rewards involved when selecting a bond mutual fund. The major bond fund categories and the recent performance records of each category are listed below. Although many bond funds share the same objectives, no two are exactly alike. Some funds invest entirely in fixed-income securities, while others, such as balanced funds, may invest a portion of their assets in common stocks.

FIGURE 16.1 Risk Summary

Type of Fund	Interest Rate Risk	Income Risk	Credit Risk	Prepayment/ Call Risk
Short-term U.S. Treasury	Low	High	Negligible	Negligible
Short-term Government	Low	High	Very Low	Low
Short-term Corporate	Low	High	Low	Negligible
Intermediate-term U.S. Treasury	Medium	Medium	Negligible	Negligible
Ginnie Mae (GNMA)	Medium	Medium	Negligible	High
Intermediate-term Corporate	Medium	Medium	Low	Low
Long-term U.S. Treasury	High	Low	Negligible	Negligible
Long-term Corporate	High	Low	Low	Medium

Diversified bond funds generally seek high current income and often also seek capital appreciation. These funds are more flexible than other bond funds, with the ability to invest across a variety of fixed-income sectors. These sectors include investment-grade and high-yield corporate bonds, U.S. Treasuries, mortgage-backed securities, foreign bonds, and convertible securities. Most funds in other categories are either restricted to one or two of these sectors or are not permitted to invest in the riskier bond sectors, such as high-yield and foreign bonds.

Average Annual Total Return Through December 31, 1994

3 Years	5 Years	10 Years
5.4%	7.9%	9.7%

Government funds seek current income by investing in a variety of U.S. Treasury and government agency securities, including U.S. Treasury bonds, federally guaranteed mortgage-backed securities, and other government notes. Treasury securities are exempt from state and local taxes and considered free from the risk of default.

Average Annual Total Return Through December 31, 1994

3 Years	5 Years	10 Years
3.5%	6.4%	8.7%

Government Mortgage-Backed Funds typically seek high current income consistent with capital preservation. These funds hold securities that represent ownership interest in home mortgage loans that are issued or guaranteed by government agencies. Only those mortgages backed by the Government National Mortgage Association (Ginnie Mae) are backed by the full faith and credit of the U.S. government, allowing Ginnie Maes the same high-quality standing as U.S. Treasuries. These securities carry prepayment risk.

Average Annual Total Return Through December 31, 1994

3 Years	5 Years	10 Years
2.5%	6.0%	8.21%

High-yield corporate bond funds seek high current income and typically invest at least two-thirds of their portfolios in lower-rated corporate bonds (BBB or lower). In return for a generally higher yield, investors must accept a greater degree of risk than for funds invested in higher-rated bonds.

Average Annual Total Return Through December 31, 1994

3 Years	5 Years	10 Years
9.9%	10.2%	9.8%

Income funds with an equity kicker typically seek to provide reasonable income and capital growth, plus conservation of principal. Such funds will invest in a diversified portfolio of securities including bonds, convertible securities, preferred stocks, and common stocks.

Balanced funds usually have a three-part investment objective. They seek to conserve investor's initial principal, pay current income, and achieve long-term growth of both principal and income. Balanced funds include bonds, preferred stocks and common stocks in their portfolios.

Average Annual Total Return Through December 31, 1994

3 Years	5 Years	10 Years
5.0%	7.6%	11.2%

Convertible funds generally seek a high level of total return through a combination of income and capital growth. Funds in this category invest in bonds and stocks that can be exchanged by the investor for common stock in the issuing company. This investment offers the opportunity for capital appreciation from the underlying common stock. However, because they sell at a premium to the conversion value of the stock, convertibles usually offer lower yields than similar quality nonconvertibles.

Average Annual Total Return Through December 31, 1994

3 Years	5 Years	10 Years
8.2%	8.8%	10.4%

Flexible funds may seek current income, capital appreciation, or a combination of the two. These funds are generally free to invest in any type of security, including U.S. government obligations, mortgage-backed securities, corporate debt securities, U.S. bank obligations, obligations of state and local governments, asset-backed securities, convertible securities, *and common and preferred stocks.*

Average Annual Total Return Through December 31, 1994

3 Years	5 Years	10 Years
5.6%	8.3%	11.1%

International bond funds generally seek a high level of income by investing in the debt securities of companies and countries throughout the world, including the United States. As a secondary objective, many funds in this group also seek preservation and possible enhancement of capital. Funds in this group normally invest at least 65 percent of their assets in debt securities issued by foreign governments and corporations. Funds in this group are sometimes referred to as "world" or "global" bond funds.

Average Annual Total Return Through December 31, 1994

3 Years	5 Years	10 Years
3.3%	6.6%	10.2%

Investment-grade corporate bond funds seek a high current income consistent with capital preservation and generally keep at least 65 percent of total assets in investment-grade (BBB or higher) fixed-income securities.

Average Annual Total Return Through December 31, 1994

3 Years	5 Years	10 Years
4.4%	7.0%	8.9%

National municipal bond funds invest in bonds issued by states and municipalities to finance airports, bridges, highways, hospitals, schools, water and sewer works, and other public projects. Generally, income earned on these securities is not subject to taxation by the federal government, but may be taxed under state and local laws. For some taxpayers, portions of income earned on these funds may be subject to the federal alternative minimum tax.

Average Annual Total Return Through December 31, 1994

3 Years	5 Years	10 Years
4.5%	6.2%	8.4%

Single-state municipal bond funds work just like national municipal bond funds except their portfolios contain the issues of just one state. A resident of that state has the advantage of receiving income exempt from both federal and state tax. The income from these funds may also be subject to the federal alternative minimum tax for some taxpayers. There are single-state funds for many of the fifty states.

Average Annual Total Return Through December 31, 1994

3 Years	5 Years	10 Years
4.7%	6.3%	8.1%

Getting Your Bond'$ Worth!

Whether your needs are short- or long-term, you'll find that there are many types of fixed-income mutual funds, each with its own unique set of characteristics. Since bond funds come in a broad variety and have a range of objectives, look for funds that share your personal investment objectives and tolerance for risk.

17

☆ ☆ ☆ ☆ ☆ ☆ ☆ ☆ ☆ ☆ ☆ ☆ ☆ ☆ ☆ ☆ ☆

Reaching Your Investment Goals with Government Bond Funds

☆ ☆ ☆ ☆ ☆ ☆ ☆ ☆ ☆ ☆ ☆ ☆ ☆ ☆ ☆ ☆ ☆

Conservative, income-oriented investors frequently turn to the government bond fund group to meet their investment objectives. Government bond funds generally manage their portfolios in an effort to produce steady income, maximize total return, and preserve shareholders' capital. To achieve this, government funds primarily invest in securities issued by the U.S. Treasury and government agencies, commonly acknowledged as the safest securities in the world because they are backed by the U.S. government. Of course, *government bond mutual fund shares* themselves are not backed by the U.S. government.

The U.S. government is the world's largest borrower, with over $3 trillion of U.S. Treasury securities outstanding. To meet its needs, the U.S. Treasury offers a variety of investment opportunities—combining predictable income with security and specific tax advantages. Because payment of interest and principal is guaranteed by the full faith and credit of the U.S. government, Treasuries are considered the highest quality of all bonds. However, in exchange for offering this very high margin of credit safety, Treasuries carry the lowest yields. See Chapter 2, U.S. Treasury Bonds, for more on Treasury instruments.

When choosing a government bond fund, the temptation is to go after the fund offering the highest yield. But that may not be the best way to achieve your investment goals. The choice of a fund should depend on your reasons for investing and your personal time frame.

For instance, if you're investing to receive income, remember that even as bond fund prices fall in reaction to a rise in interest rates, the reduced values may be offset by higher yields to help you earn the income you need. Look for funds that may offer the level of income you need at the level of risk (from interest-rate fluctuations) you are ready to accept. A fund with a longer average maturity may fluctuate too much for investors with short time horizons, while one with a shorter average maturity may not yield enough to produce sufficient returns for investors with long time horizons. If your investment time frame is one year or less, you may want to consider a government money market fund rather than a bond fund.

The chart below indicates the risk/reward tradeoff for investors with different time horizons.

Time Horizon	*Risk/Reward Tradeoff*
Less than one year	Yields may be lower than other fixed-income investments, but principal mains intact.
From one to five years	Yields can be higher than money market funds, though prices fluctuate, especially if interest rates move.
From five to ten years	Income is higher, but prices are more sensitive to interest-rate movements.
More than ten years	Potential return is highest on your investment, but prices may be highly volatile.

Government bond funds are offered at three basic maturity levels: short-term, intermediate-term, and long-term. The following descriptions may help when you consider which type of government fund can provide the investment characteristics you need.

Short-term government funds invest primarily in short-term U.S. Treasury bills, notes, and bonds, and U.S. government agency securities, with an average maturity of 1 to 3 years.

Intermediate-term government funds invest primarily in U.S. Treasury and agency securities with an average maturity of 5 to 10 years. These funds are exposed to a higher degree of principal risk, due to changes in interest rates, than a short-term fund.

Long-term government bond funds invest primarily in long-term U.S. Treasury bonds and agency securities. Such funds are well-suited for investors who seek relatively consistent income without worry of credit risk, although share prices will fluctuate significantly with changes in interest rates due to the long-term nature of the funds' holdings.

Investment Performance

As a group, government bond funds have fared quite well over longer time periods. The group produced an average annual return of 8.7 percent for the ten years ending December 31, 1994. However, as interest rates fluctuated during that time, there were wide swings in total return from year to year. For instance, following total returns of 21.9 percent in 1985 and 15 percent in 1986, the group produced a 0.0 percent return in 1987. In 1994, the average return was -3.7 percent, after an 8.6 percent return in 1993.

FIGURE 17.1   Government Bond Funds Group versus Lehman Brothers Aggregate Bond Index

	Group Return (%)	LEH AGI Return (%)		Group Return (%)	LEH AGI Return (%)
1985	21.9	22.1	1990	7.8	8.3
1986	15.0	15.3	1991	14.1	16.0
1987	0.0	2.7	1992	5.9	7.5
1988	6.8	7.9	1993	8.6	9.8
1989	12.4	14.6	1994	-3.7	-2.1

Average Annual Total Return for Different Periods
Ending December 31, 1994

	Group (%)	LEH AGI (%)
1 Year	-3.6	-2.1
3 Years	2.5	4.9
5 Years	6.0	7.7
10 Years	8.2	10.0

Figure 17.1 indicates historical average annual total returns for each year from 1985 to 1994, and for different periods ending in 1994, of the government bond fund group and the Lehman Brothers Aggregate Bond Index (LEH AGI).

A Recommended Government Bond Fund

Strong Government Securities Fund
1000 Heritage Reserve
Menomenee Falls, WI 53051
800-368-1030

Portfolio manager: Bradley Tank   *Min. initial investment:* $1,000
Dividends payable: Monthly   *Min. subsequent investment:* $50
Sales fee: None   *Date of inception:* October 29, 1986
Expense ratio: 0.90%   *Net assets (1/95):* $267 million

Investment Objective

Strong Government Securities Fund's objective is to provide a high level of current income.

Investment Policy

To achieve its objective, the fund has a fundamental policy of investing at least 80 percent of its assets in U.S. government securities under normal market conditions. The balance of assets may be invested in other investment-grade fixed-income securities. The fund does not invest in non-investment-grade securities.

Fixed-income securities the fund may invest in include: (i) corporate debt securities, including bonds, debentures, and notes; (ii) bank obligations, such as certificates of deposit, banker's acceptances, and time deposits; (iii) commercial paper; (iv) repurchase agreements; private placements (restricted securities); debt securities issued by foreign issuers; (v) convertible securities; (vi) preferred stocks; (vii) U.S. government securities; and (viii) mortgage-backed securities, collateralized mortgage obligations, and similar securities.

Fund Expenses

The following table illustrates the expenses and fees you would incur as a shareholder of Strong Government Securities Fund. These expenses and fees are subject to change.

Shareholder transaction expenses

Sales load imposed on purchases:	None
Sales load imposed on reinvested dividends:	None
Deferred sales charges:	None
Redemption fees:	None
Exchange fees:	None

Annual fund operating expenses

Investment management fee	0.60%
12b-1 fees	None
Other expenses	0.36
Total operating expenses	0.96%

Since there is no cost to buy shares in Strong Government Securities Fund, all your money goes to work for you. The fund's total operating expenses are about the same as those of the average government bond fund.

Performance

Since its inception in 1986, Strong Government Securities Fund consistently has been one of the top performers in its group. Figure 17.2 indicates annual total returns for the fund for each full year of operation ending December 31 and comparative results of the government bond fund group. This is followed by total returns and the growth of $10,000 invested in the fund for different periods ending December 31, 1994 (assuming automatic reinvestment of income and capital gains distributions).

Investment Income

The fund's dividends from ordinary income are declared daily and distributed monthly. Net realized capital gains, if any, are distributed annually. Shareholders may receive distributions in cash or have them reinvested in additional shares of the fund.

Figure 17.3 indicates the annual income and percentage yield you would have received each year if you had made a $10,000 investment in the fund, at the beginning of January 1987, assuming that you reinvested capital gains distributions in additional fund shares. Shares owned are as of the beginning of each year and reflect reinvestment of any capital gains distributions paid in the previous year.

The value of the original $10,000 investment on January 1, 1995 was 11,149 dollars. The fund was able to increase slightly the value of investors' principal during the seven years, while producing an average dividend yield of 7.4 percent.

FIGURE 17.2   Strong Government Securities Fund versus Government Bond Fund Group.

	Fund Return (%)	Group Return (%)		Fund Return (%)	Group Return (%)
1987	3.4	0.0	1991	16.7	14.1
1988	10.5	6.8	1992	9.2	5.9
1989	9.9	12.4	1993	12.7	8.6
1990	8.7	7.8	1994	-3.4	-3.7

	Fund Return (%)	Growth of $10,000
1 Year	-3.4	$ 9,660
3 Years	6.0	11,910
5 Years	8.6	15,106

FIGURE 17.3 Annual Income and Yield on $10,000 Invested in Strong
Government Securities Fund

	Shares Owned	Annual Income	Yield (%)		Shares Owned	Annual Income	Yield (%)
1987	991	$644	6.4	1991	1,010	$778	7.8
1988	991	674	6.7	1992	1,026	821	8.2
1989	1,000	800	8.0	1993	1,074	709	7.1
1990	1,006	785	7.9	1994	1,116	700	7.0

Comments

Strong Government Securities Fund is designed primarily for investors who seek higher yields than money market funds generally offer and the low credit risk that U.S. government securities carry, but who are willing to accept some principal fluctuation in order to achieve that objective.

The fund seeks high current income and invests in various securities backed by the U.S. Government and its agencies. Recently, about half the fund's assets were invested in mortgage-backed securities, evenly split between basic pass-through bonds and more complex collateralized mortgage obligations. At times, the manager has added municipal bonds to the portfolio when high yields from those tax-exempt securities have warranted the move.

The fund will further diversify as conditions permit, for example, by taking positions in corporate bonds. Management does not attempt to make prepayment bets regarding the mortgage-backed issues the fund owns, but it will sometimes use principal-only and interest-only strips, generally in combination, to limit their risky characteristics. Strips are U.S. Treasury bonds that have been separated into their principal and interest components, which are then traded separately.

The Strong Government Security Fund's negative return in 1994, a tough year for virtually all fixed-income funds, was slightly better than its peers. Longer-term, its three- and five-year ranks are close to the top of the government funds group. This actively managed fund is a solid choice for investors averse to credit risk and who want to avoid a high level of volatility.

3 Other Top-Performing Government Bond Funds

During the five-year period ending in 1994, the following three other mutual funds characterized as government bond funds were leaders in their group in total return. No-load funds in this list that can be purchased directly from the mutual fund companies are listed with an asterisk.

Fund	Five-Year Average Annual Total Return (%)
*Heartland U.S. Government Securities Fund	8.6
*T. Rowe Price U.S. Treasury Intermediate Fund	8.0
Advantage Government Securities Fund	8.0

Following are addresses, phone numbers, and investment performance for each fund. The charts show the year-by-year total return and dividend yield of the funds from 1990 to 1994.

*Heartland U.S. Government Securities Fund
790 North Milwaukee Street
Milwaukee, WI 53202
800-432-7856

Dividends payable: Monthly   **Min. initial investment:** $1,000
Max. sales load: None
Max. redemption fee: 3.0%   **Date of inception:** April 9, 1987
Expense ratio: 1.06%   **Net assets:** $65 million

Investment Results 1990–1994

	Total Return (%)	Dividend Yield (%)		Total Return (%)	Dividend Yield (%)
1990	10.0	7.9	1993	17.8	6.4 .
1991	17.0	7.5	1994	-9.6	6.7
1992	10.1	7.3			

*T. Rowe Price U.S. Treasury Intermediate Fund
100 East Pratt Street
Baltimore, MD 21202
800-225-5132

Dividends paid: Monthly   *Minimum initial investment:* $2,500
Maximum sales load: None   *Date of inception:* September 29, 1989
Expense ratio: 0.70%   *Net assets:* $176 million

Investment Results 1990–1994

	Total Return (%)	Dividend Yield (%)		Total Return (%)	Dividend Yield (%)
1990	9.0	8.1	1993	8.0	5.5
1991	14.8	6.6	1994	-2.2	6.1
1992	6.3	6.0			

Advantage Government Securities Fund
280 Trumbull Street
Hartford, CT 06103
800-241-2039

Dividends paid: Monthly   *Minimum initial investment:* $500
Maximum sales load: 4.0%   *Date of inception:* February 1, 1986
Expense ratio: 1.30%   *Net assets:* $159 million

Investment Results 1990–1994

	Total Return (%)	Dividend Yield (%)		Total Return (%)	Dividend Yield (%)
1990	8.6	8.1	1993	19.0	5.4
1991	14.7	7.5	1994	-9.6	6.4
1992	9.8	6.6			

Getting Your Bond'$ Worth!

If you are a conservative, income-oriented investor, consider funds that primarily invest in securities issued by the United States Treasury and government agencies. Such bonds are commonly acknowledged as the safest securities in the world. Government bond funds generally manage their portfolios in an effort to produce steady income, maximize total return, and preserve shareholders' capital.

18

☆ ☆ ☆ ☆ ☆ ☆ ☆ ☆ ☆ ☆ ☆ ☆ ☆ ☆ ☆ ☆ ☆ ☆

Finding Top Performers in Government Mortgage-Backed Bond Funds

☆ ☆ ☆ ☆ ☆ ☆ ☆ ☆ ☆ ☆ ☆ ☆ ☆ ☆ ☆ ☆ ☆ ☆

Government mortgage-backed bond funds have long been purchased by investors seeking above average income. The average yield for funds in this group was 6.2 percent in late 1994. These funds hold securities that represent ownership interest in home mortgage loans. The vast majority are issued or guaranteed by government agencies. Only those bonds issued by the Government National Mortgage Association (Ginnie Mae) are backed by the full faith and credit of the U.S. government, allowing Ginnie Maes the same high-quality standing as U.S. Treasuries.

These bonds carry *prepayment* risk, the risk that a bond issuer may decide to pay off the principal of an existing bond before it matures. Prepayment risk is a special concern with mortgage-backed bonds such as Ginnie Maes. During periods when interest rates are low and many mortgage-backed bonds are being prepaid (because homeowners are refinancing), both the yield and the share price of a mortgage-backed bond fund may drop within a short period of time. This is because the fund must reinvest its assets at the prevailing rate, which is always lower during times when widespread prepayments are occurring. Because of this potential risk, Ginnie Maes offer higher yields than U.S. Treasuries.

You may want to avoid government mortgage-backed bond funds if you believe that interest rates may fall significantly in the future and you are not planning to invest for a long enough time period to endure low interest-rate environments. A security backed by the full faith and credit of the United States is guaranteed only as to the timely payment of interest and principal when held to maturity. The current market prices for such securities are not guaranteed and will fluctuate.

As an illustration of interest rate risk, the chart below depicts the effect of one and two percentage point changes in interest rates on an intermediate-term bond (10-year maturity) yielding 5.5 percent at par.

Percentage Change in the Price of a Bond Yielding 5.5%

	Percentage Price Change Resulting from	
	Increase in Interest Rates (%)	*Decrease in Interest rates (%)*
1 Percentage Point Change	-7.3	+8.0
2 Percentage Points Change	-13.9	+16.7

Portfolio Holdings

Government mortgage-backed bond funds generally invest at least 65 percent of their assets in U.S. agency-backed mortgage securities. The bulk of these securities are Government National Mortgage Association (GNMA or Ginnie Mae) pass-through certificates. Ginnie Mae pass-through certificates are mortgage-backed securities representing part ownership of a pool of mortgage loans. Monthly mortgage payments of both interest and principal "pass through" from homeowners to certificate investors, such as the government mortgage-backed funds. These funds reinvest the principal portion in additional securities and distribute the interest portion as income to fund shareholders. The mortgage loans underlying Ginnie Mae certificates—issued by lenders such as mortgage bankers, commercial banks, and savings and loan associations—are either insured by the Federal Housing Administration (FHA) or guaranteed by the Veterans Administration (VA). Each pool of mortgage loans must be approved by the Government National Mortgage Association, a U.S. government corporation within the U.S. Department of Housing and Urban Development.

Although stated maturities on Ginnie Mae certificates generally range from 25 to 30 years, effective maturities are usually much shorter due to the prepayment of the underlying mortgages by homeowners. On average, Ginnie Mae certificates are repaid within 12 years and so are classified as intermediate-term securities.

Other mortgage-backed securities held by funds in this group include the Federal National Mortgage Association (FNMA or Fannie Mae) and the Federal Home Loan Mortgage Corporation (FHLMC or Freddie Mac). The balance of these funds' portfolios, that which is not invested in mortgages, will typically be comprised of U.S. government or agency-issued securities. To reduce sensitivity to bond price depreciation, some funds keep their maturities in the short to intermediate range.

Investment Performance

Like most bond funds, the government mortgage-backed funds group experience difficulties in periods of rising interest rates, the most recent of which took place in 1994. With a dividend yield of 7.0 percent and a decline in value of 10.6 percent, the average fund in this group had a total return in 1994 of -3.6 percent (total return = dividend yield plus or minus change in value).

Over the long run, however, the group has done quite well. Figure 18.1 indicates historical average annual total returns for each year from 1985 to 1994, and for different periods ending in 1994, of the government mortgage-backed bond fund group and the Lehman Brothers Aggregate Bond Index (LEH AGI), an index of more than 6,000 debt securities.

FIGURE 18.1 Government Mortgage-Backed Bond Funds Group versus Lehman Brothers Aggregate Bond Index

	Group Return (%)	LEH AGI Return (%)		Group Return (%)	LEH AGI Return (%)
1985	19.1	22.1	1990	9.3	8.3
1986	11.0	15.3	1991	13.4	16.0
1987	2.4	2.7	1992	5.7	7.5
1988	7.5	7.9	1993	5.7	9.8
1989	12.8	14.6	1994	-3.6	-2.1

Average Annual Total Return for Different Periods Ending December 31, 1994

	Group (%)	LEH AGI (%)
1 Year	-3.6	-2.1
3 Years	2.5	4.9
5 Years	6.0	7.7
10 Years	8.2	10.0

A Recommended Government Mortgage-Backed Bond Fund

Vanguard Fixed-Income Securities Fund GNMA Portfolio
P.O. Box 2600
Valley Forge, PA 19482
800-662-7447

Portfolio manager: Paul Kaplan
Investment adviser: Wellington Management Company
Dividends payable: Monthly
Sales fee: None
Expense ratio: 0.28%

Min. initial investment: $3,000 (additional: $100)
Date of inception: June 27, 1980
Net assets as of November, 1994: $6 billion

Investment Objective

Vanguard Fixed Income Securities Fund GNMA Portfolio is a no-load fund that seeks to provide investors with a high level of current income consistent with the maintenance of principal and liquidity.

Investment Policy

The GNMA Portfolio invests at least 80 percent of its assets in Government National Mortgage Association pass-through certificates. The balance of the portfolio's assets may be invested in other U.S. Treasury or U.S. government agency securities, as well as in repurchase agreements collateralized by such securities. The portfolio may also invest in bond (interest rate) futures and options to a limited extent.

Fund Expenses

The following table illustrates the expenses and fees you would incur as a shareholder of the fund. These expenses and fees are subject to change.

Shareholder transaction expenses

Sales load imposed on purchases:	None
Sales load imposed on reinvested dividends:	None
Redemption fees:	None
Exchange fees:	None

Annual fund operating expenses

Management & administration expenses:	0.21%
Investment advisory fees:	0.02
12b-1 fees	None
Other expenses	
Distribution costs	0.03
Miscellaneous expenses	0.02
Total operating expenses	0.28

Since there is no cost to buy shares in the Vanguard GNMA Portfolio, all your money goes to work for you. Further, the very low operating expenses of the fund enhances its long-term investment performance. These operating expenses are less than a third of those incurred by the average fund in the group.

Performance

In the past ten years, the Vanguard GNMA Portfolio has been a consistent performer, with an average total annual return of 9.5 percent for the period, versus 8.2 percent for the group.

Figure 18.2 indicates annual total returns for the portfolio for each full year of operation ending December 31 and comparative results of the government mortgage-backed bond funds group. This is followed by total returns and the growth of $10,000 invested in the portfolio for different periods ending December 31, 1994 (assuming automatic reinvestment of income and capital gains distributions).

Investment Income

Dividends consisting of virtually all of the ordinary income of the GNMA Portfolio are paid to shareholders on the first business day of each month. Net capital gains distributions, if any, are made annually. Dividend and capital gains distributions may be reinvested in additional shares or received in cash.

Figure 18.3 indicates the annual income and percentage yield you would have received each year if you had made a $10,000 investment, in the beginning of January 1985, assuming that capital gains distributions were reinvested in additional shares of the fund.

FIGURE 18.2 Vanguard Fixed-Income Securities Fund GNMA Portfolio versus Government Mortgage-Backed Bond Funds Group

	Fund Return (%)	Group Return (%)		Fund Return (%)	Group Return (%)
1985	20.7	19.1	1990	10.3	9.3
1986	11.7	11.0	1991	16.8	13.4
1987	2.1	2.4	1992	6.9	5.7
1988	8.8	7.5	1993	5.9	5.7
1989	14.8	12.8	1994	-1.0	-3.6

	Fund Return (%)	Growth of $10,000
1 Year	-1.0	$ 9,900
3 Years	3.8	11,184
5 Years	7.6	14,423

The value of the original $10,000 investment on January 11, 1995, was $10,385. The fund was able to increase slightly the value of investors' principal during the ten years, but income from dividends dropped steadily, reflecting an environment of generally declining interest rates. The one-share increase in total shares owned occurring in 1988 resulted from the reinvestment of a small capital gain.

Comments

Manager Paul Kaplan generally uses about 80 percent of the fund's assets to purchase GNMA certificates. The remainder of the assets are normally invested in U.S. Treasury or other agency securities though the fund has authority to invest in bond futures and options on futures to a limited extent. Depending on current market conditions, Mr. Kaplan expects that the fund will maintain a defensive strategy that includes low average coupon rates. During 1994, it sold off some of its high-coupon securities, which were dragging its performance down.

Vanguard Fixed-Income GNMA Portfolio has long been one of the top-performing mortgage funds. Since its inception in 1980, it has underperformed its peers only once, in 1987, and then by a narrow margin. The fund is especially attractive because of its extremely low expense structure.

FIGURE 18.3   Annual Income and Yield on $10,000 Invested in Vanguard GNMA Portfolio

	Shares Owned	Annual Income	Yield (%)		Shares Owned	Annual Income	Yield (%)
1985	1,083	$1,170	11.7	1990	1,084	$921	9.2
1986	1,083	1,072	10.7	1991	1,084	911	9.1
1987	1,083	964	9.6	1992	1,084	856	8.6
1988	1,084	954	9.5	1993	1,084	705	7.1
1989	1,084	954	9.5	1994	1,084	700	7.0

3 Other Top Performing Government Mortgage-Backed Bond Funds

During the ten-year period ending in 1994, the following three other mutual funds characterized as government mortgage-backed bond funds were leaders in their group in total return. The funds in this list can be purchased through investment brokers.

	Ten-Year Average Fund Annual Total Return %
Kemper U.S. Government Securities Fund	**9.3**
Van Kampen Merritt U.S. Government Fund	**9.1**
Alliance Mortgage Securities Income Fund	**8.9**

Following are addresses, phone numbers, and investment performance for each fund. The charts show the year-by-year total return and dividend yield of the funds from 1985 to November 30, 1994.

Kemper U.S. Government Securities Fund A
120 South LaSalle Street
Chicago, IL 60603
800-621-1048

Dividends payable: Monthly   *Min. initial investment: $1,000*
Max. sales load: 4.5%   *Date of inception:* October 1, 1979
Expense ratio: 0.71%   *Net assets:* $5 billion

Investment Results 1985–1994

	Total Return (%)	Dividend Yield (%)		Total Return (%)	Dividend Yield (%)
1985	22.3	10.3	1990	9.7	8.9
1986	16.2	10.0	1991	17.3	8.3
1987	2.7	10.5	1992	4.6	7.9
1988	6.3	10.0	1993	6.3	6.5
1989	14.0	9.5	1994	-3.7	7.4

Van Kampen Merritt U.S. Government Fund
1 Park View Plaza
Oakbrook Terrace, IL 60181
800-225-2222

Dividends payable: Monthly   *Min. initial investment:* $1,000
Max. sales load: 4.65%   *Date of inception:* May 31, 1984
Expense ratio: 0.93%   *Net assets:* $3.1 billion

Investment Results 1985–1994

	Total Return (%)	Dividend Yield (%)		Total Return (%)	Dividend Yield (%)
1985	22.1	11.4	1990	9.6	8.8
1986	14.0	10.4	1991	15.8	8.3
1987	1.4	9.7	1992	6.3	8.3
1988	7.5	8.5	1993	8.0	7.8
1989	13.9	8.6	1994	-5.1	8.2

Alliance Mortgage Securities Income Fund
1345 6th Avenue
New York, NY 10105
800-969-2438

Dividends payable: Monthly   *Min. initial investment:* $250
Max. sales load: 3.0%   *Date of inception:* February 29, 1984
Expense ratio: 0.96%   *Net assets:* $682 million

Investment Results 1985–1994

	Total Return (%)	Dividend Yield (%)		Total Return (%)	Dividend Yield (%)
1985	18.4	11.8	1990	11.0	9.6
1986	11.2	10.4	1991	15.4	9.1
1987	3.5	10.7	1992	7.7	8.6
1988	8.6	10.8	1993	10.1	7.2
1989	11.0	10.7	1994	-6.1	7.1

Getting Your Bond'$ Worth!

Government mortgage-backed bond funds have long been purchased by investors seeking above average income. Such funds hold securities that represent ownership interest in home mortgage loans, the vast majority of which are either issued or guaranteed by government agencies, allowing them the same high-quality standing as U.S. Treasuries.

19

☆ ☆ ☆ ☆ ☆ ☆ ☆ ☆ ☆ ☆ ☆ ☆ ☆ ☆ ☆ ☆ ☆

Achieving Premium Yields for Aggressive Investors—High-Yield Corporate Bond Funds

☆ ☆ ☆ ☆ ☆ ☆ ☆ ☆ ☆ ☆ ☆ ☆ ☆ ☆ ☆ ☆ ☆

High-yield corporate bond funds offer you a way to invest in the high-risk junk bond market by pursuing both capital growth and high income. Long-term growth opportunities can be found in the securities of companies in the midst of restructuring or even bankruptcy but with comeback potential. Securities of such companies sell at low levels. So, if the rebound measures of the companies are successful, the securities are likely to increase in value—leading to capital appreciation for those who invested at low prices.

Aggressive bond fund investors have been paying attention to the solid performance of mutual funds that invest in junk bonds. High-yield corporate bond funds generally endeavor to produce high current income and capital growth for their shareholders. These funds invest in carefully selected lower-quality bonds that offer premium yields to compensate for the risk of price volatility, default, and untimely payment of principal and interest. For appreciation potential, high-yield funds focus on securities issued by distressed or troubled companies they believe to have good comeback potential.

High-yield bond funds have been through a dramatic series of events over the last several years. In 1989 and 1990, many investors deserted high-yield funds, when they encountered double-digit losses. As mutual fund shares were sold, managers were forced to sell into weakness to meet redemptions, pushing depressed bond prices even lower.

A spectacular comeback came in 1991, thanks to strong demand for higher-yielding issues and improving corporate balance sheets. Bond prices soared, causing the average high-yield fund to gain more than 35 percent for the year. While the group hasn't lost all its excitement, it has toned down a bit. Double-digit returns of more than 16 percent were turned in by the group in both 1992 and 1993. Then rising interest rates resulted in a negative total return for 1994, with a group of average of -3.8 percent.

For the future, many portfolio managers are cautiously optimistic. They believe the default rate on high-yield bonds should remain low as long as the economy does not deteriorate. And while yield spreads have narrowed considerably from their peak of nearly 1,000 basis points, high-yield bonds still offer about 300 basis points more than the ten-year Treasury bond (100 basis points equal one percentage point).

During 1994, a difficult time for bond funds, performance of high-yield bond funds was heavily determined by sector allocation. In particular, funds benefited from exposure to cyclical (economically sensitive) companies, especially those in commodity-linked industries like paper and forest products, metals and mining, and chemicals. Despite very low inflationary pressures, commodities prices soared, a great benefit to material producers and sellers. At the other end of the spectrum, some of the previous year's favorites, such as emerging markets and gaming, were hurt by adverse market forces.

Most leading funds moved into high-yielding, lower-grade debt. The high coupons of such securities (up to 15 percent and higher) made them far less sensitive to rate fluctuations than most. Even though there is a greater risk of default in this area, bonds with stable credit backing (relative to their ratings) generally trade at a premium, paying their coupons and thus generating positive monthly dividends.

Corporate high-yield funds look good for the near future. Total returns from these funds will consist mostly of dividend income rather than price gains. If you are interested in high-yield funds, look first at those funds that are not being overly exposed to shaky credit risk. A slowing of economic growth in the United States could lead to accelerating defaults.

Investment Performance

Over the last decade, the high-yield corporate bond group has led all other domestic taxable bond fund groups in total return. Only international bond funds had a slightly better performance, and then only for the full ten years. Nevertheless, it was often a rocky road that led the high-yield corporate funds to their leadership position, swinging from low or negative returns in 1987, 1989, 1990, and 1994 to a high of more than 35 percent in 1991.

Figure 19.1 indicates historical average annual total returns for each year from 1985 to 1994, and for different periods ending in 1994, of the high-yield corporate bond fund group and the Lehman Brothers Aggregate Bond Index (LEH AGI).

FIGURE 19.1 High-Yield Corporate Bond Funds Group versus Lehman Brothers Aggregate Bond Index

	Group Return (%)	LEH AGI Return (%)		Group Return (%)	LEH AGI Return (%)
1985	21.3	22.1	1990	-9.6	8.3
1986	13.1	15.3	1991	35.2	16.0
1987	2.0	2.7	1992	16.4	7.5
1988	12.7	7.9	1993	16.6	9.8
1989	-0.2	14.6	1994	-3.8	-2.1

**Average Annual Total Return for Different Periods
Ending December 31, 1994**

	Group (%)	LEH AGI (%)
1 Year	-3.8	-2.1
3 Years	9.9	4.9
5 Years	10.2	7.7
10 Years	9.8	10.0

A Recommended High-Yield Corporate Bond Fund

Fidelity Capital and Income Fund
82 Devonshire Street
Boston, MA 02109
800-544-8888

Portfolio manager: David Breazzano   *Min. initial investment:* $2,500
Dividends payable: Monthly   (additional: $250)
Sales fee: None   *Date of inception:* November 1, 1977
Expense ratio: 0.97%   *Net assets as of January, 1995:*
                                            $2.5 billion

Investment Objective

Fidelity Capital & Income Fund seeks to provide a combination of income and capital growth.

Investment Policy

The fund may invest in any combination of debt and securities, but focuses on lower-rated debt securities and securities of companies with uncertain financial positions, which present higher risks of untimely interest and principal payments, default, and price volatility than higher-rated securities, and may present problems of liquidity and valuation.

The fund follows an aggressive investment program, and may invest in any type or quality of debt or equity security that the fund's manager judges to have the potential for income or capital growth. The fund has no fixed policy as to the allocation of its assets between debt and equity investments. However, management anticipates that the fund will invest the majority of its assets in bonds and other interest-bearing debt instruments, with particular emphasis on lower-rated debt securities (which may be in default). The fund may make investments solely for the purpose of earning income or solely for capital gains, in keeping with its objective of providing shareholders with a combination of income and capital growth.

The success of the fund's aggressive investment style depends on the manager's financial analysis and research, particularly with respect to investments in companies experiencing financial difficulties.

Fund Expenses

The following table illustrates the expenses and fees you would incur as a shareholder of Fidelity Capital & Income Fund. These expenses and fees are subject to change.

Shareholder transaction expenses

Sales load imposed on purchases:	None
Sales load imposed on reinvested dividends:	None
Deferred sales charges:	None
Redemption fee (for shares held less than 365 days):	1.50%
Exchange fees:	None

Annual fund operating expenses:

Investment management fee	0.71%
12b-1 fees	None
Other expenses	0.26
Total operating expenses	0.97%

Since there is no cost to buy shares in Fidelity Capital & Income Fund, all your money goes to work for you. The fund's total operating expenses are about 12 percent less than those of the average high-yield corporate bond fund.

Performance

In the last decade, Fidelity Capital & Income Fund ranked among the top performers in its group. Figure 19.2 indicates annual total returns for the fund from 1985 to 1994 and comparative results of the high-yield corporate bond fund group. This is followed by total returns and the growth of $10,000 invested in the fund for different periods ending December 31, 1994 (assuming automatic reinvestment of income and capital gains distributions).

Investment Income

The fund distributes substantially all of its net investment income and capital gains to shareholders each year. Income dividends are declared daily and paid monthly. Any net capital gains normally are distributed in June.

Figure 19.3 indicates the annual income and percentage yield you would have received each year if you had made a $10,000 investment in the fund, at the beginning of January 1985, assuming that capital gains distributions were reinvested in additional shares of the fund. Shares owned are as of the beginning of each year and reflect reinvestment of any capital gains distributions paid in the previous year.

The value of the original $10,000 investment on January 1, 1995, was $10,701. The fund was able to increase slightly the value of investors' principal during the seven years, while producing generous annual dividends.

FIGURE 19.2 Fidelity Capital & Income Fund versus High Yield Corporate Bond Fund Group.

	Fund Return (%)	Group Return (%)		Fund Return (%)	Group Return (%)
1985	25.5	21.3	1990	-4.0	-9.6
1986	18.0	13.1	1991	29.8	35.2
1987	1.3	2.0	1992	28.0	16.4
1988	12.6	12.7	1993	24.9	16.6
1989	-3.1	-0.2	1994	-5.5	-3.8

	Fund Return (%)	Growth of $10,000
1 Year	-5.5	$ 9,450
3 Years	14.5	15,011
5 Years	13.3	18,670
10 Years	11.8	30,508

FIGURE 19.3 Annual Income and Yield on $10,000 Invested in Fidelity Capital & Income Fund

	Shares Owned	Annual Income	Yield (%)		Shares Owned	Annual Income	Yield (%)
1985	1,164	$1,338	13.4	1990	1,240	$942	9.4
1986	1,164	1,280	12.8	1991	1,240	917	9.2
1987	1,201	1,261	12.6	1992	1,240	818	8.2
1988	1,240	1,240	12.4	1993	1,240	1,029	10.3
1989	1,240	1,339	13.4	1994	1,240	1,066	10.7

Comments

Fidelity Capital & Income Fund invests in carefully selected lower-quality bonds. These investments offer premium yields to compensate for the risk of price volatility, default, and untimely payment of principal and interest. In addition, for appreciation, it focuses on securities issued by distressed or troubled companies with good comeback potential.

High-yield markets offer investors possibilities for capital appreciation as well as current income, as companies strive to reduce the burden of managing debt or to recover after a restructuring. Junk bonds continue to offer high yields and can be a worthwhile source for current income. To reduce risk in the volatile lower-quality securities market, diversification is essential. This fund diversifies across broad market sectors and among an array of industries as well as individual companies.

Manager David Breazzano, when selecting low-rated bonds for inclusion in the fund, pays particular attention to so-called distressed securities, which represent companies in or close to bankruptcy. With proper research, Breazzano believes management may be able to identify distressed companies that are poised for a recovery. When that happens, the resulting bond-rating upgrades can cause a bond to appreciate substantially.

The fund is geared for the risk portion of your portfolio. Share price, yield, and return will vary, and the market for lower-quality securities may be thinner and less active than other securities markets. Further, the fund encourages investment by long-term oriented investors by imposing a 1.5 percent redemption fee on shares held less than 365 days. The fee is designed to offset the costs associated with short-term trading and is paid directly to the fund. For shares held beyond 365 days, there are no redemption fees.

Lower-rated and non-rated corporate bonds recently accounted for about 70 percent of the fund's assets. Investment-grade bonds (bonds carrying one of the four highest ratings assigned by major bond-rating services) comprised less than five percent of assets. The balance of the portfolio was invested in equities and cash-equivalent securities.

Some analysts believe that the fund's outstanding three- and five-year annualized returns are unlikely to be sustained, as the Federal Reserve Board's monetary actions could slow economic growth, to the detriment of companies strapped for cash. The fund's long-term performance relative to its peers, however, makes it an attractive choice for high-yield bond fund investors.

3 Other Top Performing High-Yield Corporate Bond Funds

During the five-year period ending in 1994, the following three other mutual funds characterized as high-yield corporate bond funds were leaders in their group in total return. These funds all carry front-end loads or redemption fees.

Fund	Five-Year Average Annual Total Return (%)
Fidelity Advisor High Yield Fund	**15.9**
Liberty High Income Bond Fund	**13.6**
Oppenheimer Champion High Yield Fund	**13.4**

Following are addresses, phone numbers, and investment performance for each fund. The charts show the year-by-year total return and dividend yield of the funds from 1990 to 1994.

Fidelity Advisor High Yield Fund
82 Devonshire Street
Boston, MA 02109
800-522-7297

Dividends payable: Monthly *Min. initial investment:* $2,500
Max. sales load: 4.75% *Date of inception:* January 5, 1987
Expense ratio: 1.22% *Net assets:* $624 million

Investment Results 1990–1994

	Total Return (%)	Dividend Yield (%)		Total Return (%)	Dividend Yield (%)
1990	7.1	12.1	1993	20.5	7.7
1991	34.9	11.5	1994	-2.1	6.7
1992	22.5	9.0			

Liberty High Income Bond Fund
Federated Tower
Pittsburgh, PA 15222
800-245-4770

Dividends payable: Monthly   **Min. initial investment:** $500
Max. sales load: 4.5%   **Date of inception:** November 30, 1977
Expense ratio: 1.18%   **Net assets:** $447 million

Investment Results 1990–1994

	Total Return (%)	Dividend Yield (%)		Total Return (%)	Dividend Yield (%)
1990	-12.8	16.7	1993	17.4	8.9
1991	60.5	11.3	1994	-1.7	9.6
1992	17.2	10.6			

Oppenheimer Champion High Yield Fund
3410 South Galena Street
Denver, CO 80231
800-525-7048

Dividends payable: Monthly   *Min. initial investment:* $1,000
Max. sales load: 4.75%   *Date of inception:* November 16, 1987
Expense ratio: 1.37%   *Net assets:* $160 million

Investment Results 1990–1994

	Total Return (%)	Dividend Yield (%)		Total Return (%)	Dividend Yield (%)
1990	2.1	13.0	1993	21.4	8.7
1991	30.5	11.9	1994	-0.1	8.2
1992	16.2	11.0			

Getting Your Bond'$ Worth!

High-yield corporate bond funds offer you a way to pursue both capital growth and high income. These funds invest in the high-risk junk bond market. For appreciation potential, high-yield funds focus on securities issued by distressed or troubled companies they believe to have good comeback potential, and that offer premium yields to compensate for the risk of price volatility and default in the payment of principal and interest.

20

☆ ☆ ☆ ☆ ☆ ☆ ☆ ☆ ☆ ☆ ☆ ☆ ☆ ☆ ☆ ☆ ☆ ☆

Getting the Best Return on Quality with Investment-Grade Corporate Bond Funds

☆ ☆ ☆ ☆ ☆ ☆ ☆ ☆ ☆ ☆ ☆ ☆ ☆ ☆ ☆ ☆ ☆ ☆

If you're safety conscious, it generally doesn't pay to go with lower quality. Since corporate bonds are not guaranteed as to the timely payment of interest and principal, it is important to look at their credit rating, if any, to assess the risk. Given that, a diversified portfolio of top-quality corporate bonds can provide the safety many investors seek while paying more income than is generally available from government securities.

Corporate bonds are issued by many types of companies in order to finance projects ranging from building a new plan to modernizing at a current location. Bonds issued by corporations with excellent credit ratings and established profitability pay lower interest due to the relatively low degree of risk. These securities can vary widely in yield and maturity. Corporate bond fund portfolio managers constantly monitor the securities within the fund, buying and selling bonds to maintain or improve the fund's share value as they seek to achieve the best return that market conditions will allow.

Investment-grade corporate bond funds generally seek to provide a high level of current income consistent with preservation of capital. Capital appreciation is a secondary consideration. Funds in this group take a conservative approach, with a high percentage of portfolio assets, usually 75 percent or more, invested in investment-grade securities (those issues carrying a credit rating of BBB or better). In

131

addition to bonds issued by U.S. corporations, such securities may include U.S. government and agency issues, and foreign government and foreign corporation securities, among others.

Investment Performance

Figure 20.1 indicates historical average annual total returns for each year from 1985 to 1994, and for different periods ending in 1994, of the investment grade corporate bond fund group and the Lehman Brothers Aggregate Bond Index (LEH AGI).

FIGURE 20.1 Investment-Grade Corporate Bond Fund Group versus Lehman Brothers Aggregate Bond Index

	Group Return (%)	LEH AGI Return (%)		Group Return (%)	LEH AGI Return (%)
1985	20.1	22.1	1990	6.8	8.3
1986	13.5	15.3	1991	15.7	16.0
1987	2.0	2.7	1992	7.0	7.5
1988	8.0	7.9	1993	10.0	9.8
1989	11.2	14.6	1994	-3.4	-2.1

**Average Annual Total Return for Different Periods
Ending December 31, 1994**

	Group Return (%)	LEH AGI Return (%)
1 Year	-3.4	-2.1
3 Years	4.4	4.9
5 Years	7.0	7.7
10 Years	8.9	10.0

A Recommended Investment-Grade Corporate Bond Fund

Harbor Bond Fund
One SeaGate
Toledo, OH 43666
800-422-1050

Portfolio manager: William Gross
Investment adviser: Harbor
  Capital Advisers, Inc.
Dividends payable: Quarterly
Sales fee: None
Expense ratio: 0.77%

Min. initial purchase: $2,000
  (additional: $500)
Date of inception: December 29, 1987
Net assets as of October, 1994:
  $165 million

Investment Objective

Harbor Bond Fund seeks to achieve maximum total return, consistent with the preservation of capital and prudent investment management through investment in an actively managed portfolio of fixed-income securities.

Investment Policy

Under normal conditions, the fund invests at least 65 percent of its assets in bonds, such as:

- obligations issued or guaranteed by the U.S. government and its agencies, with maturities of at least five years; obligations issued or guaranteed by a foreign government or its agencies, or by supra-national organizations (such as the International Bank for Reconstruction);
- obligations of domestic or foreign corporations and other entities (rated Baa or better by Moody's or BBB or better by Standard & Poor's, or if unrated, determined by management to be of comparable quality); and
- mortgage-related and other asset-backed securities.

Depending on the level of interest rates, the average maturity of these securities will vary between 8 and 15 years.

In selecting securities for Harbor Bond Fund's portfolio, the manager utilizes economic forecasting, interest-rate expectations, credit and call risk analysis and other security selection techniques. The proportion of the fund's assets invested in securities with particular characteristics (such as maturity, type, and coupon rate) may vary based on the manager's outlook for the economy, the financial markets, and other factors.

Under normal conditions, at least 60 percent of the fund's total assets will be invested in securities of U.S. issuers. The fund may not invest more than 25 percent of its assets in the securities of issuers located in any single country other than the United States.

Fund Expenses

The following table illustrates the expenses and fees you would incur as a shareholder of the fund. These expenses and fees are subject to change.

Shareholder transaction expenses

Sales load imposed on purchases:	None
Sales load imposed on reinvested dividends:	None
Redemption fees:	None
Exchange fees:	None

Annual fund operating expenses

Management Fee	0.45%
Other expenses	0.32
Total operating expenses	0.77

Since there is no cost to buy shares in the Harbor Bond Fund, all your money goes to work for you. Further, the fund's reasonable operating expenses should not be a hindrance to its long-term investment performance. These operating expenses are about 12 percent less than those incurred by the average fund in the investment-grade corporate bond fund group.

Performance

For the five years ending in 1994, the Harbor Bond Fund had a steady performance record, with an average total annual return of 8.8 percent for the period, versus 7.0 percent for its peer group.

Figure 20.2 indicates annual total returns for the fund for each full year of operation and comparative results of the investment-grade corporate bond funds group. This is followed by total returns and the growth of $10,000 invested in the portfolio for different periods ending in 1994 (assuming automatic reinvestment of income and capital gains distributions).

Investment Income

Dividends consisting of virtually all of the ordinary income of the Harbor Bond Fund are distributed to shareholders quarterly. Net capital gains distributions, if any, are declared and paid annually on or about the close of the calendar year. Dividend and capital gains distributions may be reinvested in additional shares or received in cash.

Figure 20.3 indicates the annual income and percentage yield you would have received each year if you had made a $10,000 investment, in the beginning of January 1988, assuming that any capital gains distributions were reinvested in additional shares of the fund.

The value of the original $10,000 investment was $11,400 on January 1, 1995, an increase of $1,400 over the seven-year period. Income from dividends fluctuated, but averaged 7.8 percent. The 109-share increase in total shares owned resulted from reinvesting capital gains distributions that were made in five of the seven years.

FIGURE 20.2 Total Annual Returns of Harbor Bond Fund versus the Investment Grade Corporate Bond Funds Group

	Fund Return (%)	Group Return (%)		Fund Return (%)	Group Return (%)
1988	7.2	8.0	1992	9.1	7.0
1989	13.7	11.2	1993	12.4	10.0
1990	7.9	6.8	1994	-3.8	-3.4
1991	19.7	15.7			

	Fund Return (%)	Growth of $10,000
1 Year	-3.8	$ 9,620
3 Years	5.7	11,809
5 Years	8.8	15,246

Comments

Harbor Bond Fund has one of the most diversified portfolios among funds in the investment-grade corporate bond group. Its holdings are spread among several classes of income-producing securities, including investment-grade corporate bonds and notes, mortgage related securities, U.S. government obligations, and to a limited extent foreign bonds and other securities. Recently, 44 percent of the fund was invested in fixed-rate and floating-rate mortgage-backed debt. In less secure instruments, the fund held one-fifth of its assets in corporate issues, about one half of which were investment grade with the remainder in high-yield bonds. The high-yield market tends to be influenced more by equity values than by changing interest rates. In 1994, a year of rising rates, junk bond issues outperformed investment-grade bonds and helped the Harbor Bond Fund's return.

The fund seeks to achieve its goal of capital preservation and strong total return through investment in a wide range of securities. The largest concentration will generally be in AAA-rated government or government-insured debt. This may be mortgage-backed, Treasury, or debt issued by foreign governments (recently the fund held about 3 percent of its assets in foreign securities). The fund typically holds a smaller portion of assets in a broad spectrum of corporate issues with credit qualities ranging from AAA to BB.

Harbor Bond Fund is not the most conservative fund in the investment-grade corporate bond group, but it has done a pretty good job of protecting investors from losses in bad times and a better job than most of its peers at generating yield and capital gains in good times.

FIGURE 20.3 Annual Income and Yield on $10,000 Invested in Harbor Bond Fund

	Shares Owned	Annual Income	Yield (%)		Shares Owned	Annual Income	Yield (%)
1988	1,000	$670	6.7	1992	1,039	$769	7.7
1989	1,007	836	8.4	1993	1,062	690	6.9
1990	1,016	864	8.6	1994	1,109	742	7.4
1991	1,016	874	8.7				

3 Other Top Performing Investment-Grade Corporate Bond Funds

During the five-year period ending in 1994, the following three mutual funds categorized as investment-grade corporate bond funds were leaders in their group in total return. One fund in this list that is no-load and can be purchased directly from the mutual fund company is listed with an asterisk.

Five-Year Average Fund Annual Total Return (%)

*Nations Managed Bond Trust	**10.2**
FPA New Income Fund	**10.2**
Alliance Corporate Bond Fund	**9.9**

Following are addresses, phone numbers, and investment performance for each fund. The charts show the year-by-year total return and dividend yield of the funds from 1990 to 1994.

*Nations Managed Bond Trust
101 South Tryon Street
Charlotte, NC 28255
800-982-2271

Dividends payable: Monthly   *Min. initial investment:* $1,000
Max. sales load: None   *Date of inception:* September 19, 1989
Expense ratio: 0.72%   *Net assets:* $172 million

Investment Results 1990–1994

	Total Return (%)	Dividend Yield (%)		Total Return (%)	Dividend Yield (%)
1990	15.4	15.8	1993	10.7	5.8
1991	23.0	14.7	1994	-7.6	5.4
1992	7.2	6.5			

FPA New Income Fund
11400 West Olympic Boulevard
Los Angeles, CA 90006
800-638-3060

Dividends payable: Quarterly   *Min. initial investment:* $1,500
Max. sales load: 4.50%   *Date of inception:* January 1, 1969
Expense ratio: 0.74%   *Net assets:* $123 million

Investment Results 1990–1994

	Total Return (%)	Dividend Yield (%)		Total Return (%)	Dividend Yield (%)
1990	8.4	7.5	1993	10.2	5.8
1991	18.8	7.7	1994	3.1	7.9
1992	11.1	6.2			

Alliance Corporate Bond Fund
1345 6th Avenue
New York, NY 10105
800-969-2438

Dividends paid: Monthly   *Min. initial investment:* $250
Max. sales load: 4.25%   *Date of inception:* March 1, 1974
Expense ratio: 1.30%   *Net assets:* $229 million

Investment Results 1990–1994

	Total Return (%)	Dividend Yield (%)		Total Return (%)	Dividend Yield (%)
1990	5.5	10.4	1993	31.1	7.2
1991	18.1	8.5	1994	-13.3	8.5
1992	13.3	9.3			

Getting Your Bond'$ Worth!

Safety-conscious investors can look to investment grade corporate bond funds for a diversified portfolio of top-quality corporate and government bonds. These funds seek to provide a high level of current income consistent with preservation of investors' capital and pay more income than is generally available from government securities alone.

21

Lowering Your Risk
with Diversified
Bond Funds

If you are risk-averse and seeking investments with a higher rate of return compared to other fixed income securities, you may want to consider mutual funds that are classified as *diversified bond funds*. Funds in this category generally seek to provide investors with high current income. Capital preservation and long-term growth are often listed as secondary objectives. Diversified bond funds have the ability to invest across a variety of fixed-income sectors. These sectors include investment-grade and high-yield corporate bonds, U.S. Treasuries, mortgage-backed securities, foreign bonds, and convertible bonds.

Over the long term, diversified bond funds have outperformed most other fixed-income categories. The added flexibility that funds in this group possess has allowed them to participate fully in the bond market rallies of the last several years. Diversified bond funds have also been less volatile than many other fixed-income funds, mainly due to their broad diversification across bond sectors.

Investment Performance

Figure 21.1 indicates historical average annual total returns for each year from 1985 to 1994, and for different periods ending in 1994, of the diversified bond fund group and the Lehman Brothers Aggregate Bond Index (LEH AGI).

FIGURE 21.1 Diversified Bond Group versus Lehman Brothers
Aggregate Bond Index

	Group Return (%)	LEH AGI Return (%)		Group Return (%)	LEH AGI Return (%)
1985	24.6	22.1	1990	2.0	8.3
1986	13.0	15.3	1991	21.1	16.0
1987	4.6	2.7	1992	8.6	7.5
1988	11.5	7.9	1993	13.7	9.8
1989	7.4	14.6	1994	-4.4	-2.1

**Average Annual Total Return for Different Periods
Ending December 31, 1994**

	Group (%)	LEH AGI (%)
1 Year	-4.4	-2.1
3 Years	5.4	4.9
5 Years	7.9	7.7
10 Years	9.7	10.0

A Recommended Diversified Bond Fund

Janus Flexible Income Fund
100 Fillmore Street
Denver, CO 80206
800-525-3713

Portfolio manager:
  Ronald V. Speaker
Dividends payable: Monthly
Sales fee: None
Expense ratio: 0.93%

Min. initial purchase: $1,000
  (additional: $50)
Date of inception: July 2, 1987
Net assets as of October, 1994:
  $391 million

Investment Objective

Janus Flexible Income Fund is a no-load mutual fund that seeks to
maximize total return, consistent with preservation of capital.

Investment Policy

The Flexible Income Fund pursues its objective primarily through
investments in income-producing securities. Total return is expected to

result from a combination of current income and capital appreciation, although income will normally be the dominant component of total return. The fund invests at least 80 percent of its assets in income-producing securities.

The fund may invest in a wide variety of income-producing securities including corporate bonds and notes, government securities, preferred stock, income-producing common stocks, debt securities that are convertible or exchangeable into equity securities, and debt securities that carry with them the right to acquire equity securities through warrants. The fund may hold securities of any maturity and quality and the average maturity and quality of its portfolio may vary substantially.

Further, the fund may invest in foreign securities, including those of corporate and government issuers. It may also invest in high-yield/high-risk bonds and may have substantial holdings in such securities.

Fund Expenses

The following table illustrates the expenses and fees you would incur as a shareholder of the fund. These expenses and fees are subject to change.

Shareholder transaction expenses

Sales load imposed on purchases:	None
Sales load imposed on reinvested dividends:	None
Redemption fees:	None
Exchange fees:	None

Annual fund operating expenses

Management Fee	0.62%
Other expenses	0.31
Total operating expenses	0.93

Since there is no cost to buy shares in the Janus Flexible Income Fund, all your money goes to work for you. Further, the fund's reasonable operating expenses should not be a hindrance to its long-term investment performance. These operating expenses are about 20 percent less than those incurred by the average fund in the group.

Performance

Since its inception in 1987, the Janus Flexible Income Fund has been a strong performer. In the five years ending in 1994, it produced an average total annual return of 8.6 percent for the period, versus 7.9 percent for the group.

Figure 21.2 indicates annual total returns for the fund for each full year of operation ending in 1994 and comparative results of the diversified bond funds group. This is followed by total returns and the growth of $10,000 invested in the portfolio for different periods ending in 1994 (assuming automatic reinvestment of income and capital gains distributions).

Investment Income

Dividends consisting of virtually all of the ordinary income of the Janus Flexible Income Fund are paid to shareholders as of the last business day of each month. Net capital gains distributions, if any, are declared and paid annually in December. Dividend and capital gains distributions may be reinvested in additional shares or received in cash.

FIGURE 21.2 Total Annual Returns of Janus Flexible Income Fund versus the Diversified Bond Funds Group

	Fund Return (%)	Group Return (%)		Fund Return (%)	Group Return (%)
1988	10.7	11.5	1992	11.9	8.6
1989	4.1	7.4	1993	15.7	13.7
1990	-4.6	2.0	1994	-2.9	-4.4
1991	26.0	21.1			

	Fund Return (%)	Growth of $10,000
1 Year	-2.9	$9,710
3 Years	7.9	12,562
5 Years	8.6	15,106

Figure 21.3 indicates the annual income and percentage yield you would have received each year if you had made a $10,000 investment, in the beginning of January 1988, assuming that any capital gains distributions were reinvested in additional shares of the fund.

The value of the original $10,000 investment on January 1, 1995, was $9,327. The fund was not able to maintain the value of investors' principal through the entire seven years. Income from dividends also dropped, reflecting an environment of generally declining interest rates. The 35-share increase in total shares owned resulted from the reinvestment of capital gains distributions made in 1989, 1992, and 1993. An additional capital gains distribution made at the end of 1994 added 27 more shares, resulting in a total of 1,066 shares owned at the beginning of 1995.

Comments

Janus Flexible Income Fund's holdings are diversified among several classes of income-producing securities, including high-yield and investment-grade corporate bonds, preferred stocks, and dollar-based foreign bonds. The fund occasionally holds high cash positions as a commitment to capital preservation, a primary objective of the fund.

FIGURE 21.3   Annual Income and Yield on $10,000 Invested in Janus Flexible Income Fund

	Shares Owned	Annual Income	Yield (%)		Shares Owned	Annual Income	Yield (%)
1988	1,008	$927	9.3	1992	1,037	$830	8.3
1989	1,010	980	9.8	1993	1,037	798	8.0
1990	1,018	926	9.3	1994	1,039	810	8.1
1991	1,018	733	7.3				

During the period of rising interest rates in 1994, a difficult time for bond funds, Flexible Income Fund's defensive cash position contributed to its outperforming other players in the diversified bond fund group by 150 basis points (1 1/2 percentage points).

Despite the negative publicity that has surrounded derivatives, the fund has utilized bond futures as a means to reduce the fund's interest rate risk. The manager has stressed that his use of bond futures is purely a hedging device, and not a speculative interest-rate bet like those used by many of his peers.

Management attributes the fund's strong relative performance to its flexible investment guidelines, which do not mandate specific investments. Though Janus Flexible Income Fund has the flexibility to invest in several asset classes, it is primarily a bond fund. Overall economic and market outlook determines the fund's asset allocation between government and corporate bonds, being more aggressive in healthy markets and conservative during periods of tough market conditions, as was the case in 1994.

Since assuming control of the fund in 1990, manager Ronald Speaker has obtained consistently strong returns as indicated by the fund's performance in the last three years. The Flexible Income Fund is a solid choice as a diversified bond holding for risk-averse investors seeking exposure to various income-producing securities worldwide.

3 Other Top Performing Diversified Income Bond Funds

During the five-year period ending in 1994, the following three mutual funds categorized as diversified bond funds were leaders in their group in total return. A fund in this list that can be purchased directly from the mutual fund company is listed with an asterisk.

Fund	Five-Year Average Annual Total Return (%)
Oppenheimer Strategic Income Fund	9.8
Putnam Diversified Income Fund	9.8
*MAS Funds Fixed Income Portfolio	8.7

Following are addresses, phone numbers, and investment performance for each fund. The charts show the year-by-year total return and dividend yield of the funds from 1990 to 1994.

Oppenheimer Strategic Income Fund
3410 South Galena Street
Denver, CO 80231
800-525-7048

Dividends payable: Monthly   *Min. initial investment:* $1,000
Max. sales load: 4.75%   *Date of inception:* October 16, 1989
Expense ratio: 0.99%   *Net assets:* $3 billion

Investment Results 1990–1994

	Total Return (%)	Dividend Yield (%)		Total Return (%)	Dividend Yield (%)
1990	7.8	11.8	1993	19.5	8.6
1991	20.3	10.4	1994	-4.4	9.0
1992	7.7	8.7			

Putnam Diversified Income Fund
One Post Office Square
Boston, MA 02109
800-225-1581

Dividends payable: Quarterly   *Min. initial investment:* $500
Max. sales load: 5.75%   *Date of inception:* October 3, 1988
Expense ratio: 0.88%   *Net assets:* $1.5 billion

Investment Results 1990–1994

	Total Return (%)	Dividend Yield (%)		Total Return (%)	Dividend Yield (%)
1990	5.0	9.7	1993	15.9	6.0
1991	23.6	8.2	1994	-5.6	8.3
1992	12.3	7.8			

*MAS Funds Fixed Income Portfolio
1 Tower Bridge
West Conshohocken, PA 19428
800-354-8185

Dividends payable: Quarterly   *Min. initial investment:* $2,500
Max. sales load: None   *Date of inception:* November 1, 1984
Expense ratio: 0.48%   *Net assets:* $1.2 billion

Investment Results 1990–1994

	Total Return (%)	*Dividend Yield (%)*		*Total Return (%)*	*Dividend Yield (%)*
1990	7.2	8.3	1993	13.8	7.3
1991	21.3	8.4	1994	-5.4	5.7
1992	8.7	7.4			

Getting Your Bond'$ Worth!

If you are risk-averse and are seeking investments with a higher rate of return compared to other fixed income securities, consider diversified bond funds. This group of bond funds have outperformed most other fixed-income categories over the long run. The added flexibility that funds in this group possess has allowed them to participate fully in bond market rallies and be less volatile than many other fixed-income funds.

22

☆ ☆ ☆ ☆ ☆ ☆ ☆ ☆ ☆ ☆ ☆ ☆ ☆ ☆ ☆ ☆ ☆ ☆

Investing in the Whole Bond Market— Bond Index Funds

☆ ☆ ☆ ☆ ☆ ☆ ☆ ☆ ☆ ☆ ☆ ☆ ☆ ☆ ☆ ☆ ☆ ☆

Once available only to institutional investors, such as pension fund managers, individuals are now able to invest in a replication of the whole bond market, or in segments of the market by buying shares in a single fund. Today, index investing is an investment strategy of choice among both institutions and individuals, with hundreds of billions of dollars invested in index funds nationwide.

The term *indexing* describes an investment approach that seeks to parallel the investment returns of a specific stock or bond market benchmark, or index. An indexing approach reduces the impact of the unpredictable and inevitable ups and downs of individual securities. The investment manager attempts to replicate the investment results of the target index by holding all (or a representative sample in the case of very large indexes) of the securities in the index. There is no effort made to actively manage the portfolio or to make bets on individual securities or narrow industry sectors in an attempt to outpace the index. Rather, indexing is a passive approach emphasizing broad diversification and low portfolio trading activity.

The foundation of bond indexing is based on a simple truth: it is impossible for all fixed-income securities investors in the aggregate to have superior performance compared to the overall market. According to Ibbotson Associates, since 1926 the bond market has had an average return of 5 percent per year. Since 1980, yields have been much higher. For instance, the total return on 10-year U.S. Treasury bonds has been 11 percent. Some investors, as a result of luck or skill, have earned more than the average, while others have earned less. But the historical return is, by definition, the average amount that all bond investors in different periods have been able to achieve as a group.

But those average returns are gross, before expenses (such as management fees, commissions and other costs). Net returns can be significantly less, resulting in a number well below the market return. Most mutual funds have costs in the form of advisory fees, distribution charges, operating expenses and portfolio transaction costs. According to Lipper Analytical Services, these costs, on average, total approximately 2 percent of investor assets. In contrast, one of the main advantages of an index bond fund should be its low cost. A properly run index fund should pay no advisory fees (since there is no active investment management), should keep operating expenses at a very low level, and should keep portfolio transactions costs at a minimum. The lower the expenses a fund incurs, the closer will be the fund's performance to the index it tracks.

Figure 22.1 shows the five- and ten-year total returns (income plus capital change) through 1994 of bond fund groups compared with the Lehman Brothers Aggregate Bond Index, an index of more than 6,000 bonds that includes U.S. Treasury and agency securities, corporate bonds, and mortgage-backed securities.

FIGURE 22.1   Average Annual Returns of Bond Fund Groups for Five and Ten Year Periods Ending in 1994

	Average Annual Return (%)	
Group (%)	**5 Years**	**10 Years**
Diversified Bond Funds	7.9	9.7
Government Bond Funds	6.4	8.7
Government Mortgage-Backed Bond Funds	6.0	8.2
High-Yield Corporate Bond Funds	10.2	9.8
Investment-Grade Corporate Bond Funds	7.0	8.9
International Bond Funds	6.6	10.2
Lehman Brothers Aggregate Bond Index	7.7	10.0

Investing in Index Bond Funds

An index bond fund invests in fixed-income securities in an attempt to match the investment performance of a distinct market index. The use of index funds achieves its advantage over the long term.

Indexing's main appeal is to long-term investors who seek a very competitive investment return through broadly diversified portfolios. Index bond funds provide investors with a high degree of relative predictability in an uncertain bond market. Nothing can assure absolute returns, but index fund investors can feel confident that their investment should not dramatically underperform other funds investing in the same type of securities and, over the long term, index funds should deliver a very competitive relative performance.

Investors wanting to buy into particular segments of the fixed-income securities market now have an increasing selection of bond index funds to choose from. For example, The Vanguard Group, long-time leader in index funds, offers the following four portfolios that seek to replicate specific market sectors of the unmanaged Lehman Brothers Aggregate Bond Index:

1. *Total Bond Market Portfolio.* This tracks the performance of the total universe of investment-grade bonds as measured by the Lehman Brothers Aggregate Bond Index.
2. *Short-Term Bond Portfolio.* With an average maturity of two to three years, it invests more than 80 percent of its assets in U.S. government bonds (including mortgage-backed securities) and the remainder in investment-grade corporate bonds.
3. *Intermediate-Term Bond Portfolio.* With an average maturity of seven to ten years, it invests approximately 66 percent of its assets in U.S. government bonds and the remainder in investment-grade corporate bonds.
4. *Long-Term Bond Portfolio.* With an average maturity of 20 to 25 years, it invests approximately 66 percent of its assets in U.S. government bonds and the remainder in investment-grade corporate bonds.

You will find more information on these and other bond index funds later in this chapter.

A Recommended Bond Index Fund

Vanguard Bond Index Fund— Total Bond Market Portfolio
P.O. Box 2600
Valley Forge, PA 19482
800-662-7447

Portfolio Manager:
  Ian McKinnon
Dividends payable: Monthly
Sales fee: None
Expense ratio: 0.18%

Min. initial investment:
  $3,000 (additional: $100)
Date of inception: December 11, 1986
Net assets as of October, 1994:
  $1.9 billion

Investment Objective

The Total Bond Market Portfolio seeks to replicate the performance of the Lehman Brothers Aggregate Bond Index (Aggregate Bond Index), a broad index which encompasses three major classes of investment-grade fixed-income securities in the United States:

1. U.S. Treasury and agency securities;
2. corporate bonds; and
3. mortgage-backed securities, with maturities greater than one year.

Investment Policy

The Total Bond Market Portfolio is not managed according to traditional methods of "active" investment management, which involve the buying and selling of securities based upon economic, financial, and market analyses and investment judgment. Instead, the portfolio, utilizing a "passive" or "indexing" investment approach, attempts to duplicate the investment performance of the Aggregate Bond Index through statistical sampling procedures. The portfolio invests in a group of fixed-income securities selected from its index which, when taken together, are expected to perform similarly to the index as a whole. This sampling technique is expected to enable the portfolio to trace interest income and price movements of the index, while minimizing brokerage, custodial and accounting costs. The portfolio is managed without regard to tax ramifications.

Recently, the portfolio held 53 percent of its assets in U.S. Treasury and agency securities, 19 percent in corporate bonds and 28 percent in mortgage-backed securities. The average maturity of the securities held was 8.9 years. Fixed-income securities have been primarily of investment-grade quality, that is, rated at least BBB by Standard & Poor's Corporation.

In its effort to duplicate the investment performance of the index, the portfolio invests in fixed-income securities in accordance with its relative proportion of the index's total market value. These investments include U.S. Treasury and agency securities, mortgage-backed securities and corporate debt. The portfolio may also invest of to 20 percent of its assets in short-term money market instruments, and may invest in bond (interest rate) futures contracts and options to a limited extent. Such securities are held only to invest uncommitted cash valances, to maintain liquidity to meet shareholder redemptions, or to minimize trading costs. The portfolio intends to remain fully invested, to the extent practicable, in a pool of securities which will duplicate the investment characteristics of the index.

Fund Expenses

The following table illustrates the expenses and fees you would incur as a shareholder of Vanguard Bond Index Fund—Total Bond Market Portfolio. These expenses and fees are subject to change.

Shareholder transaction expenses

Sales load imposed on purchases:	None
Sales load imposed on reinvested dividends:	None
Deferred sales charges:	None
Redemption fees:	None
Exchange fees:	None

Annual fund operating expenses

Investment management fee	0.13%
12b-1 fees	None
Other expenses	0.05
Total operating expenses	0.18%

Since there is no cost to buy shares in the Total Bond Market Portfolio, all your money goes to work for you. The fund's total operating expenses are about 80 percent *less* than those of the average bond fund.

Performance

During its short history, the Total Bond Market Portfolio has come close in most years to meeting its objective of matching the Lehman Brothers Aggregate Bond Index (LEH AGI). Figure 22.2 indicates annual total returns for the portfolio during its full years of operation from 1987 to 1994 and comparative results of the Aggregate Bond Index. This is followed by total returns and the growth of $10,000 invested in the portfolio for different periods ending December 31, 1994 (assuming automatic reinvestment of income and capital gains distributions).

FIGURE 22.2 Vanguard Bond Index Fund—Total Bond Market Portfolio versus Lehman Brothers Aggregate Bond Index.

	Fund Return (%)	LEH AGI Index (%)		Fund Return (%)	LEH AGI Index (%)
1987	1.1	2.8	1991	15.2	16.0
1988	7.3	7.9	1992	7.1	7.4
1989	13.6	14.5	1993	9.7	9.7
1990	8.6	9.0	1994	-2.7	-2.9

	Fund Return (%)	Growth of $10,000
1 Year	-2.7	$9,730
3 Years	4.6	11,444
5 Years	7.4	14,289

Investment Income

Dividends consisting of virtually all of the ordinary income of the portfolio are declared daily and are paid on the first business day of each month. Capital gains distributions, if any, are made annually.

Figure 22.3 indicates the annual income and percentage yield you would have received each year if you had made a $10,000 investment in the Total Bond Market Portfolio, at the beginning of January 1987, assuming that capital gains distributions were reinvested in additional shares of the fund. Shares owned are as of the beginning of each year and reflect reinvestment of any capital gains distributions paid in the previous year.

The value of the original $10,000 investment on January 1, 1995 was $9,436, decreasing somewhat over the eight-year period. Reflecting a gradual decline in interest rates, the portfolio's income dividends also decreased during the period.

Comments

The Total Bond Market Portfolio of the Vanguard Bond Index Fund posted a total return of -2.7 percent in 1994, but bested its investment-grade bond fund peers. The average investment-grade corporate bond fund had a return of -3.4 percent in that year, government funds were -3.7 percent, and mortgage-backed government funds were -3.6 percent. For the five-year period, Vanguard's 7.6 percent return also was significantly better than any of the three peer groups.

FIGURE 22.3 Annual Income and Yield on $10,000 Invested in Vanguard Total Bond Market Portfolio

	Shares Owned	Annual Income	Yield (%)		Shares Owned	Annual Income	Yield (%)
1987	1,006	$839	8.4	1991	1,006	$771	7.7
1988	1,006	811	8.1	1992	1,008	703	7.0
1989	1,006	802	8.0	1993	1,017	642	6.4
1990	1,006	801	8.0	1994	1,029	632	6.3

The fund is passively managed and holds nearly 1,500 separate issues. A computer-driven sampling technique is used to select the portfolio of securities so that it is representative of the sector weightings, coupon, maturity, effective duration, and credit quality of the Lehman Brothers Aggregate Bond Index. Management believes its sampling technique substantially duplicates the income and capital returns of the index.

The risk associated with the fund is essentially equal to that of the index. There is very little credit risk, since over half of the index's securities are government- or mortgage-backed issues, and all corporate securities held are investment-grade. The fund's interest rate is moderate; its average maturity generally ranges between 8.5 and 9.5 years.

The Total Bond Market Portfolio is a straightforward, low-cost investment choice for investors seeking broad fixed-income exposure. It has successfully met its objective of providing investors with returns in line with its benchmark index. If you are considering the fund, though, you should have a long-term investment horizon, as indexing demands a certain level of discipline, especially in bear markets.

Bond Index Funds and the Market Indexes They Target

Mutual fund companies have established bond funds that track a number of market indexes, both in the U.S. and overseas. Because expenses account for most of the difference between an index fund's returns and those generated by the target index, you should take special note of the operating expenses of any index fund you consider for purchase.

Some of the companies offering bond index funds are listed below, with the bond indexes targeted by each fund.

Bond Index Funds   Target Index

Fidelity Investments
82 Devonshire Street
Boston, MA 02109
800-544-8888

Fidelity U.S. Bond Index Portfolio   Lehman Brothers Aggregate
Bond Index

Galaxy Funds
440 Lincoln Street
Worcester, MA 01653
800-628-0414

Galaxy II U.S. Treasury Index Fund   U.S. Treasury Index

Portico Mutual Funds
270 East Buffalo Street
Milwaukee, WI 53202
800-228-1024

Portico Bond IMMDEX Fund   Lehman Government/
Corporate Bond Index

Portico Intermediate Bond Market   Lehman Brothers Intermediate
Government/Corporate
Bond Index

Portico Short-Term Bond Market   Lehman Brothers 1-3 Year
Government/Corporate
Bond Index

SEI Index Funds
680 E. Swedesford Road
Wayne, PA 19087-1658
800-342-5734

SEI Bond Index Portfolio   Salomon Brothers Investment
Grade Bond Index

**The Vanguard Group of
Investment Companies**
P.O. Box 2600
Valley Forge, PA 19482
800-662-7447

Vanguard Balanced Index Fund	Wilshire 5000 Index & Lehman Brothers Aggregate Bond Index
Vanguard Bond Index Fund	
Total Bond Market Portfolio	Lehman Brothers Aggregate Bond Index
Short-Term Bond Portfolio	Lehman Brothers Mutual Fund Short (1-5) Government/ Corporate Index
Intermediate-Term Bond Portfolio	Lehman Brothers Mutual Fund Intermediate (5-10) Government/Corporate Index
Long-Term Bond Portfolio	Lehman Brothers Mutual Fund Long (10+) Government/ Corporate Index

---

Getting Your Bond'$ Worth!

You can choose to invest in the whole bond market, or in important segments of the market, by buying shares in a single "index" fund. Index funds emphasize broad diversification and low portfolio trading activity by investing in a replication of the entire bond market. Index investing has become an investment strategy of choice among both institutions and individuals, with hundreds of billions of dollars invested in index funds nationwide.

23

☆ ☆ ☆ ☆ ☆ ☆ ☆ ☆ ☆ ☆ ☆ ☆ ☆ ☆ ☆ ☆ ☆ ☆

Investing Throughout the World—International Bond Funds

☆ ☆ ☆ ☆ ☆ ☆ ☆ ☆ ☆ ☆ ☆ ☆ ☆ ☆ ☆ ☆ ☆ ☆

International bond funds invest in the debt securities of companies and countries throughout the world, including the United States. They generally seek current income for their shareholders, while attempting to protect principal. International funds also are sometimes called global or world bond funds.

About half the value of the world's bonds trade in markets abroad. At times, foreign bond markets outperform our own, with higher current income, greater price appreciation, or both. These can be compelling reasons to add an international bond fund to your investment portfolio. In 1987, the average international bond fund posted a total return of 17.8 percent, compared with a total return of 2.7 percent for the average U.S. corporate bond fund. The reverse can also be true, such as in 1989 when the average U.S. corporate bond fund returned 14.6 percent to investors, compared with 5.8 percent for international bond funds.

Currency fluctuations are a concern for investors in funds that hold foreign securities. For example, the European currency crisis in 1992 aggravated an already difficult year for international bond investors. Shares of the average international bond fund in that year gained just 2.2 percent, trailing the domestic bond market by more than 5 percentage points. International investors cannot avoid these risks. But through active portfolio management, fund managers can help reduce the impact such risks can have on your investment.

The following chart illustrates how interest rates for ten-year prime government bond issues of different countries can differ from those in the United States and from each other. The yields are as of December 30, 1993 and are expressed in U.S. dollars.

Average Yields of 10 Year Prime Government Issues

Country	Yield (%)
Australia	6.68
Canada	6.61
Italy	8.66
Japan	3.25
Spain	8.09
Sweden	7.02
United Kingdom	6.18
United States	**5.75**

Investment Performance

At times, rising interest rates have weighed heavily on the international bond markets. After a strong showing in 1993, when international funds as a group turned in an impressive 13.5 percent gain, they had a disappointing performance in 1994, closing the year with a negative 5 percent showing.

Long-term investors have fared well, though, with a 10.2 percent average annual return for the ten years ending December 31, 1994. This was better than any of the other fixed-income funds (not including bond funds with equity kickers). Figure 23.1 indicates historical average annual total returns for each year from 1985 to 1994, and for different periods ending in 1994, of the international bond fund group and the Lehman Brothers Aggregate Bond Index (LEH AGI).

FIGURE 23.1   International Bond Funds Group versus Lehman Brothers
Aggregate Bond Index

	Group Return (%)	LEH AGI Return (%)		Group Return (%)	LEH AGI Return (%)
1985	25.5	22.1	1990	11.6	8.3
1986	16.6	15.3	1991	12.1	16.0
1987	17.8	2.7	1992	2.2	7.5
1988	5.2	7.9	1993	13.5	9.8
1989	5.8	14.6	1994	-5.0	-2.1

**Average Annual Total Return for Different Periods
Ending December 31, 1994**

	Group (%)	LEH AGI (%)
1 Year	-5.0	-2.1
3 Years	3.3	4.9
5 Years	6.6	7.7
10 Years	10.2	10.0

A Recommended International Bond Fund

Scudder International Bond Fund
Two International Place
Boston, MA 02110
800-225-2470

Portfolio managers: Adam Greshin
and Lawrence Teitelbaum
Dividends payable: Monthly
Sales fee: None
Expense ratio: 1.28%

Min. initial purchase: $1,000
(additional: $100)
Date of inception: July 6, 1988
Net assets as of January, 1995:
$1.2 billion

Investment Objective

Scudder International Bond Fund is a no-load mutual fund which
seeks income primarily by investing in high-grade bonds denominated
in foreign currencies. As a secondary objective, the fund seeks protec-

tion and possible enhancement of principal value by actively managing currency, bond market and maturity exposure and by security selection.

Investment Policy

To achieve its objectives, the fund primarily invests in a managed portfolio of high-grade international bonds. Portfolio investments are selected on the basis of yields, credit quality, and the fundamental outlooks for currency and interest rate trends in different parts of the world, taking into account the ability to hedge a degree of currency or local bond price risk. The fund normally invests at least 65 percent of its assets in bonds denominated in foreign currencies. including bonds denominated in the European Currency Unit (ECU).

The fund's investments may include:

- debt securities issued or guaranteed by a foreign national government, its agencies, instrumentalities or political subdivisions;
- debt securities issued or guaranteed by supranational organizations (e.g. European Investment Bank, Inter-American Development Bank or the World Bank);
- corporate debt securities;
- bank or bank holding company debt securities; and
- other debt securities, including those convertible into common stock.

The fund selects its investments from a number of country and market sectors. It may substantially invest in the issuers of one or more countries and expects generally to have investments in securities of issuers from a minimum of three different countries. Under normal circumstances, the fund will invest no more than 35 percent of the value of its assets in U.S. debt securities.

Fund Expenses

The following table illustrates the expenses and fees you would incur as a shareholder of Scudder International Bond Fund. These expenses and fees are subject to change.

Shareholder transaction expenses

Sales load imposed on purchases:	None
Sales load imposed on reinvested dividends:	None
Redemption fees:	None
Exchange fees:	None

Annual fund operating expenses

Investment management fee	0.84%
12b-1 fees	None
Other expenses	<u>0.44</u>
Total operating expenses	1.28%

Since there is no cost to buy shares in the Scudder International Bond Fund, all your money goes to work for you. The fund's total operating expenses are about 15 percent lower than those of the average international bond fund.

Performance

Scudder International Bond Fund has been generally quite volatile, but has over time rewarded its shareholders for the risks incurred, having led its group in both the three- and five-year periods ending in 1994.

Figure 23.2 indicates annual total returns for the fund for each full year of operation ending December 31 and comparative results of the international bond funds group. This is followed by total returns and the growth of $10,000 invested in the fund for different periods ending December 31, 1994 (assuming automatic reinvestment of income and capital gains distributions).

Investment Income

The fund's dividends from ordinary income are declared daily and distributed monthly. Net realized capital gains, if any, are generally distributed in November or December. Shareholders may receive distributions in cash or have them reinvested in additional shares of the fund.

Figure 23.3 indicates the annual income and percentage yield you would have received each year if you had made a $10,000 investment, in the beginning of January 1989, assuming that capital gains distribu-

FIGURE 23.2 Scudder International Bond Fund versus International Bond Funds Group.

	Fund Return (%)	Group Return (%)		Fund Return (%)	Group Return (%)
1989	7.2	5.8	1992	7.6	2.2
1990	21.1	11.6	1993	15.8	13.5
1991	22.2	12.1	1994	-8.6	-5.0

	Fund Return (%)	Growth of $10,000
1 Year	-8.6	$9,140
3 Years	4.4	11,379
5 Years	11.0	16,851

FIGURE 23.3 Annual Income and Yield on $10,000 Invested in Scudder International Bond Fund

	Shares Owned	Annual Income	Yield (%)		Shares Owned	Annual Income	Yield (%)
1989	819	$860	8.6	1992	887	$940	9.4
1990	819	950	9.5	1993	929	855	8.6
1991	837	979	9.8	1994	956	860	8.6

tions were reinvested in additional shares of the fund. Shares owned each year reflect the reinvestment of any capital gains distributions paid in the previous year.

The value of the original $10,000 investment on January 11, 1995, was $11,204. The fund was able to increase slightly the value of investors' principal during the six years and income from dividends held fairly steady. A capital gains distribution paid in late 1994 resulted in a total of 888 shares owned at the beginning of 1995.

Comments

If you're looking for an easy, low cost source of monthly income, Scudder International Bond Fund provides access to attractive income opportunities throughout the world. The fund is most appropriate for long-term investors who are willing to accept the risks of international investing, such as fluctuations in currency exchange rates.

With foreign bond markets often moving independently of ours and of each other, the broad diversification of Scudder International Bond Fund decreases the chance of its holdings all moving in a negative direction at once. This strategy helps reduce your risk, while enhancing prospects for both current income and total return. Through research and active portfolio management, the fund strives to reduce the risks of currency-exchange fluctuations by continuously monitoring the portfolio's currency, maturity, and country exposure. They emphasize quality by investing primarily in high-grade bonds—mostly foreign government and government-backed securities.

Management generally employs what it terms a "value" approach to investing; that is, the fund seeks to invest in favorably priced, higher-yielding bonds in order both to garner that income and to participate in any gains available as interest rates fall. A cautionary note: while losses were essentially unavoidable in 1994's international bond market, the fund's -8.6 percent return in that year is a reminder of its downside volatility.

3 Other Top Performing International Bond Funds

During the five-year period ending in 1994, the following three other mutual funds characterized as international bond funds were leaders in their group in total return. The no-load fund in this list that can be purchased directly from the mutual fund company is listed with an asterisk.

Fund	Five-Year Average Annual Total Return (%)
*T. Rowe Price International Bond Fund	10.5
IDS Global Bond Fund	9.0
Merrill Lynch World Income Fund	9.4

Following are addresses, phone numbers, and investment performance for each fund. The charts show the year-by-year total return and dividend yield of the funds from 1990 to November 30, 1994.

*T. Rowe Price International Bond Fund
100 East Pratt Street
Baltimore, MD 21202
800-225-5132

Dividends payable: Monthly   *Min. initial investment:* $2,500
Max. sales load: None   *Date of inception:* September 10, 1986
Expense ratio: 0.99%   *Net assets:* $757 million

Investment Results 1990–1994

	Total Return (%)	Dividend Yield (%)		Total Return (%)	Dividend Yield (%)
1990	16.0	8.6	1993	19.4	6.3
1991	17.7	7.5	1994	-1.8	6.3
1992	2.9	8.5			

IDS Global Bond Fund
IDS Tower 10
Minneapolis, MN 55440
800-328-8300

Dividends payable: Quarterly   *Min. initial investment:* $2,000
Max. sales load: 5.0%   *Date of inception:* March 20, 1989
Expense ratio: 1.24%   *Net assets:* $470 million

Investment Results 1990–1994

	Total Return (%)	Dividend Yield (%)		Total Return (%)	Dividend Yield (%)
1990	13.0	8.8	1993	16.4	6.0
1991	15.3	6.6	1994	-4.9	4.7
1992	6.5	6.0			

Merrill Lynch World Income Fund
P.O. Box 45289
Jacksonville, FL 32232
800-637-3863

Dividends payable: Monthly   *Min. initial investment:* $1,000
Max. sales load: 4.0%   *Date of inception:* September 29, 1988
Expense ratio: 0.75%   *Net assets:* $350 million

Investment Results 1990–1994

	Total Return (%)	*Dividend Yield (%)*		*Total Return (%)*	*Dividend Yield (%)*
1990	9.8	16.5	1993	13.8	7.8
1991	23.4	11.4	1994	-4.1	8.3
1992	6.2	10.7			

Getting Your Bond'$ Worth!

With about half the value of the world's bonds trading in markets abroad you may find worthwhile opportunities in international bond funds. At times, foreign bond markets outperform our own—with higher current income, greater price appreciation, or both. But remember, the reverse can also be true. In some years, foreign bonds have performed much worse that those in the U.S. International bond funds provide diversification as a part of your investment portfolio.

24

☆ ☆ ☆ ☆ ☆ ☆ ☆ ☆ ☆ ☆ ☆ ☆ ☆ ☆ ☆ ☆ ☆

Bond Funds with an Equity Kicker: 1. Balanced Funds

☆ ☆ ☆ ☆ ☆ ☆ ☆ ☆ ☆ ☆ ☆ ☆ ☆ ☆ ☆ ☆ ☆

The best way to meet your long-term financial goals is to develop a properly diversified mix of stocks and bonds. Historically, common stocks have provided an investment return more than double that of bonds or cash reserves. Chapters 24 to 26 focus on three types of income funds that have the additional objective of increasing share value by including equities in their portfolios.

If you want to avoid the extremes in either the stock or bond markets, you might want to choose funds that combine equities and debt securities for one-stop diversification. Called *balanced funds,* these mutual funds seek an above average total return by investing in a relatively fixed combination of both stocks and bonds, normally holding a minimum of 25 percent in stocks and 25 percent in bonds at any time.

Balanced funds generally have a three-part investment objective: to conserve the investor's initial principal, to pay current income and to promote long-term growth of both principal and income. This goal is sought by holding a portfolio mix of bonds, preferred stocks and common stocks.

Balanced funds frequently perform in the middle of the pack. These funds do not usually try to shoot for the top of the fund charts. Rather, their goal is to provide investors with a cautious, diversified exposure to both the stock and bond markets. The result is a fairly consistent middle-of-the-road performance, which is counted as success. This objective has historically provided as much return as the typical specialized fund, but with less risk.

In recent years, funds with more conservative stock portfolios have had superior performances. These funds have been price-conscious, with heavy weightings in typical value stocks, such as financials and industrial cyclicals. Funds with large bond positions also performed well during periods of declining interest rates, when bond prices were pushed up. However, 1994 proved to be the first time in ten years that both the stock and bond markets declined together. While many equity funds recovered somewhat late in the year, most bond funds continued to lag. By the end of December of that year, the average balanced fund produced a return of -2.9 percent, trailing the S&P 500 Index by 4.5 percentage points. As a result, the better performing balanced funds were those with the least exposure to bonds and those holding the shortest maturities.

The average income yield for funds in this group was 3.0 percent in late 1994.

Investment Performance

Many top-performing balanced funds have served their shareholders well over the long term. Investors who consider risk management to be a priority should find the performance of these funds satisfying. Figure 24.1 indicates historical average annual total returns for each year from 1985 to 1994, and for different periods ending in 1994, of funds in the balanced fund group, the S&P 500 Index and the Lehman Brothers Aggregate Bond Index (LEH AGI), an index of more than 6,000 debt securities.

FIGURE 24.1 Balanced Funds Group versus the S&P 500 Index and the
Lehman Brothers Aggregate Bond Index

	S&P Group (%)	LEH 500 (%)	AGI (%)		S&P Group (%)	LEH 500 (%)	AGI (%)
1985	27.1	32.2	22.1	1990	-0.5	-3.2	8.3
1986	16.1	18.5	15.3	1991	25.2	30.6	16.0
1987	2.7	5.2	2.7	1992	7.3	7.7	7.5
1988	11.4	16.8	7.9	1993	10.7	10.1	9.8
1989	18.3	31.5	14.6	1994	-2.9	1.6	-2.1

Average Annual Total Return for Different Periods
Ending December 31, 1994

	Group (%)	S&P 500 (%)	LEH AGI (%)
1 Year	-2.9	1.6	-2.1
3 Years	5.0	6.4	4.9
5 Years	7.6	8.8	7.7
10 Years	11.2	14.5	10.0

A Recommended Balanced Fund

Dodge & Cox Balanced Fund
1 Sansome Street
San Francisco, CA 94104
415-981-1710

Portfolio manager: Team managed *Min. initial purchase:* $3,000
Dividends payable: Quarterly   (additional: $100)
Sales fee: None   *Date of inception:* June 26, 1931
Expense ratio: 0.58%   *Net assets as of October 31, 1994:*
                                                    $714 million

Investment Objective

Dodge & Cox Balanced Fund is a no-load mutual fund with the
objectives of providing shareholders with regular income, conservation of principal and an opportunity for long-term growth of principal
and income.

Investment Policy

The fund seeks to achieve its objectives by investing in a diversified portfolio of common stocks, preferred stocks and bonds. The proportions held in common and preferred stocks and bonds are revised by the managers when considered advisable in light of their appraisal of business and investment prospects. The fund's policy is to maintain no more than approximately 75 percent of its total assets in common stocks, although management may depart from a balanced position under abnormal conditions. As a general practice, bonds are held for stability of principal and income as well as for a reserve which can be used to take advantage of investment opportunities.

It is the fund's policy to invest in high quality, investment grade bonds rated in the top four rating categories by either Moody's Investors Service (Aaa, Aa, A, Baa) or Standard & Poor's Corporation (AAA, AA, A, BBB).

A substantial position will be maintained in common stocks which have a favorable outlook for long-term growth of principal and income. Prospective earnings and dividends are major considerations in these stock selections. The level of security prices and the trend of business activity are given weight in determining the total investment position of the fund in equities at any time. Individual securities are selected with an emphasis on financial strength and a sound economic background.

In an attempt to minimize unforeseen risks in single securities, the fund seeks adequate diversification. Investments in any one stock or bond issue, with the exception of U. S. government securities, are seldom in excess of 2 percent of the assets of the fund. Purchases are made with a view to long-term holding and not for short-term trading purposes. Generally, the fund invests in securities with ready markets, mainly issues listed on national securities exchanges.

The fund may not invest more than 5 percent of the value of its total assets in the securities of any one issuer except the U.S. government, nor acquire more than 10 percent of the voting securities of any one issuer. It may not concentrate investments of more than 25 percent of the value of its total assets in any one industry, nor may it borrow money except as a temporary measure for extraordinary or emergency purposes.

Composition of the fund's portfolio: In late 1994, bonds accounted for 38 percent of the fund's portfolio. 72 common stocks comprised 57 percent of the portfolio, and cash reserves 5 percent.

Fund Expenses

The following table illustrates the expenses and fees you would incur as a shareholder of the fund. These expenses and fees are subject to change.

Shareholder transaction expenses

Sales load imposed on purchases:	None
Sales load imposed on reinvested dividends:	None
Deferred sales load:	None
Redemption fees:	None
Exchange fees:	None

Annual fund operating expenses

Management fees	0.50%
12b-1 fees	None
Other expenses	0.10%
Total fund operating expenses	0.60%

A feature of the Dodge & Cox Balanced Fund and other no-load funds is that shares are sold without a sales charge. Shares may be redeemed at net asset value without any charge.

Performance

Following a period of strong results in the past, with a 14 percent average annual return for the most recent 10 years, the fund is cautious about the future. Management believes that several factors, including a low beginning price-to-earnings structure for the overall stock market and a dramatic decline in interest rates, contributed to the strong results. They believe that returns will be lower in the next ten years.

Figure 24.2 indicates annual total returns for the Portfolio for each full year of operation and comparative results of the balanced funds group. This is followed by total returns and the growth of $10,000 invested in the portfolio for different periods ending December 31, 1994 (assuming automatic reinvestment of income and capital gains distributions).

Investment Income

Quarterly dividends from net income, when available, are paid on or about the 20th day of March, June, September and December. Any capital gains distributions of net gain on sales of securities are paid in conjunction with the December and, if necessary, March quarterly payments.

Figure 24.3 indicates the results of a $10,000 investment, made at the beginning of 1985, assuming that capital gains distributions were reinvested in additional shares of the fund. Included in the chart are the annual income and percentage yield an investor would have received on the original investment.

FIGURE 24.2   Total Return of Dodge & Cox Balanced Fund versus the Balanced Funds Group

	Fund Return (%)	Group Return (%)		Fund Return (%)	Group Return (%)
1985	32.5	27.1	1990	0.9	-0.5
1986	18.8	16.1	1991	20.7	25.2
1987	7.2	2.7	1992	10.6	7.3
1988	11.5	11.4	1993	16.9	10.7
1989	23.0	18.3	1994	2.0	-2.9

Periods Ending December 31, 1994	Fund Return (%)	Growth of $10,000
1 Year	2.0	$10,200
3 Years	9.7	13,201
5 Years	9.9	16,032
10 Years	14.0	37,072

The value of the original $10,000 investment on January 1, 1995, was $22,921. The fund was able to increase substantially the value of its investors' principal during the ten years. Income from dividends more than doubled. The performance results of Dodge & Cox Balanced Fund dramatically illustrate how the growth potential of equities in a portfolio can work to offset the effects of inflation on principal and income.

Comments

Dodge & Cox Balanced Fund has earned a place in the top echelon of its peer group in both recent years and the long term. The fund's bias toward value stocks has rewarded its shareholders. Traditionally, the manager has purchased what he considers to be undervalued issues, which can often involve buying stocks that have been battered down by bad news. Sometimes the best values are found in times of great uncertainty, and the fund does not hesitate to invest in the market during broad declines as long as its research supports its actions. However, investing in depressed securities requires a long-term horizon, and this is reflected in the fund's very low turnover rate (the extent to which its portfolio is turned over during the course of a year).

The portfolio of this balanced fund is weighted toward equities and the primary focus in recent years has been on economically sensitive industries, such as technology, machinery, consumer durables, and industrial commodities. In the fixed-income portion, management has

FIGURE 24.3   Annual Income and Yield on $10,000 Invested in Dodge & Cox Balanced Fund

	Shares Owned	Annual Income	Yield (%)		Shares Owned	Annual Income	Yield (%)
1985	386	$656	6.6	1990	486	$880	8.8
1986	390	632	6.3	1991	490	862	8.6
1987	432	734	7.3	1992	494	850	8.5
1988	470	790	7.9	1993	495	822	8.2
1989	477	840	8.4	1994	507	908	9.1

increased the fund's exposure to mortgage-backed securities, which has become increasingly more attractive as their yield spreads over U.S. Treasury bonds widen.

The fund's ability to consistently outperform many of its peers has attracted many new investors. From net assets of less than $25 million in 1985, the fund has grown to more than $700 million in late 1994. Dodge & Cox Balanced has beat the balanced fund group's average return in most of the last ten years. As more investors recognize that partial-equity funds can deliver powerful returns while simultaneously limiting risk, top-ranked funds such as this one should continue to see significant inflows of new money.

3 Other Top Performing Balanced Funds

During the ten-year period ending in 1994, the following three other mutual funds categorized as balanced funds were leaders in their group in total return. Funds in this list that are no-load or low-load and can be purchased directly are listed with an asterisk.

Fund	Ten-Year Average Annual Total Return (%)
*CGM Mutual Fund	14.8
*T. Rowe Price Balanced Fund	13.3
MFS Total Return Fund	12.8

Following are addresses, phone numbers, and investment performance for each fund. The charts show the year-by-year total return and dividend yield of the funds from 1985 to 1994.

*CGM Mutual Fund
399 Boylston Street
Boston, MA 021163
800-345-4048

Dividends payable: Quarterly   *Min. initial investment:* $2,500
Max. sales load: None   *Date of inception:* November 5, 1929
Expense ratio: 0.91%   *Net assets:* $1.2 billion

Investment Results 1985–1994

	Total Return (%)	Dividend Yield (%)		Total Return (%)	Dividend Yield (%)
1985	34.5	5.0	1990	1.1	4.3
1986	25.1	3.7	1991	40.9	3.3
1987	13.7	4.3	1992	6.1	3.4
1988	3.2	5.5	1993	21.8	2.8
1989	21.7	4.0	1994	-9.7	4.1

*T. Rowe Price Balanced Fund
100 E. Pratt Street
Baltimore, MD 21202
800-225-5132

Dividends payable: Quarterly   **Min. initial investment:** $2,500
Max. sales load: None   **Date of inception:** November 29, 1938
Expense ratio: 1.00%   **Net assets:** $388 million

Investment Results 1985–1994

	Total Return (%)	Dividend Yield (%)		Total Return (%)	Dividend Yield (%)
1985	33.0	5.5	1990	7.2	6.4
1986	23.1	4.8	1991	26.3	8.1
1987	-3.4	6.7	1992	11.3	7.0
1988	9.0	5.3	1993	13.9	3.6
1989	20.7	6.6	1994	-2.1	3.8

MFS Total Return Fund
500 Boylston Street
Boston, MA 02116
800-343-2829

Dividends payable: Quarterly   **Min. initial investment:** $1,000
Max. sales load: 4.75   **Date of inception:** October 6, 1970
Expense ratio: 0.79%   **Net assets:** $1.9 billion

Investment Results 1985–1994

	Total Return (%)	Dividend Yield (%)		Total Return (%)	Dividend Yield (%)
1985	30.2	5.7	1990	-2.3	6.0
1986	19.8	5.0	1991	21.6	5.2
1987	3.5	5.4	1992	10.1	4.9
1988	15.0	5.7	1993	15.1	4.0
1989	23.1	5.3	1994	-2.8	4.1

Getting Your Bond'$ Worth!

You can avoid the extremes in either the stock or bond markets by investing in mutual funds that invest in both stocks *and* bonds. These funds hold a relatively fixed combination of equities and fixed-income securities and have done very well to protect principal during bearish markets while paying current income and promoting long-term growth of both principal and income.

25

☆ ☆ ☆ ☆ ☆ ☆ ☆ ☆ ☆ ☆ ☆ ☆ ☆ ☆ ☆ ☆ ☆ ☆

More Bond Funds with an Equity Kicker: 2. Convertible Bond Funds

☆ ☆ ☆ ☆ ☆ ☆ ☆ ☆ ☆ ☆ ☆ ☆ ☆ ☆ ☆ ☆ ☆ ☆

Convertible bond funds invest in securities that offer both fixed-income and capital appreciation potential. Convertible securities pay a fixed dividend or rate of interest and are convertible into common stock at a specified price or conversion ratio. The yield on convertibles is normally less than that of nonconvertible bonds or preferred stocks, and the potential for capital gains is less than with a common stock investment.

Convertible funds usually offer less credit risk and market risk than equity funds while providing an opportunity for investors to participate in the future success of the companies into whose common shares convertibles can be exchanged. Convertible bonds and convertible preferred stock have the same priority of claim on a corporation's earnings and assets as regular bonds and preferreds. Bonds take precedence over preferred stock, and both take precedence over common stock. For a review of convertibles, see Chapter 5, Convertible Bonds.

Consider buying convertible bond funds if your investment objective includes capital appreciation along with current income. Remember, though, because potential for growth is a key feature, yield is less than on straight bond funds. Convertible funds tend to rise in value with increasing common stock prices, so they also represent a hedge against inflation.

The popularity of convertible bond funds continues to grow. The funds were generally ignored in the late 1980s in favor of pure stock and bond funds, but many investors have taken a second look. After interest rates declined in the early 1990s, the securities market poured forth a spate of new convertibles in 1993 providing investors, hungry for yields, with a steady flow of instruments to choose from. Such heavy demand, plus a strong equity market, allowed convertible bond funds to stand out until 1994 when interest rates turned up and returns of most convertible funds were hit hard. In that year the average convertible fund had a return of -3.7 percent.

The appeal of convertible bond funds arises from their dual identity. They combine elements of both stock and bond performance, they provide income without sacrificing appreciation potential. This gives fund managers a good deal of flexibility in assembling their portfolios.

Be aware, though, that while convertible securities offer the best features of bonds and stocks, they are also subject to the difficulties of both. These securities are often at the mercy of interest-rate fluctuations, credit risk, or the failing strength of their underlying equities.

The average income yield for funds in this group was 3.6 percent in late 1994.

Investment Performance

Top-performing funds in the convertible bond group have produced excellent returns over the long term. If you are a conservative investor seeking growth and income, you should find the performance of these funds satisfying. Figure 25.1 indicates historical average annual total returns for each year from 1985 to 1994, and for different periods ending in 1994, of funds in the convertible bond fund group, the S&P 500 Index and the Lehman Brothers Aggregate Bond Index (LEH AGI).

FIGURE 25.1 Convertible Bond Funds Group versus the S&P 500 Index and the Lehman Brothers Aggregate Bond Index

	S&P Group (%)	LEH 500 (%)	AGI (%)		S&P Group (%)	LEH 500 (%)	AGI (%)
1985	23.4	32.2	22.1	1990	-6.0	-3.2	8.3
1986	15.3	18.5	15.3	1991	27.8	30.6	16.0
1987	-2.9	5.2	2.7	1992	14.3	7.7	7.5
1988	11.4	16.8	7.9	1993	15.9	10.1	9.8
1989	14.4	31.5	14.6	1994	-3.7	1.6	-2.1

Average Annual Total Return for Different Periods Ending December 31, 1994

	Group (%)	S&P 500 (%)	LEH AGI (%)
1 Year	-3.7	1.6	-2.1
3 Years	8.2	6.4	4.9
5 Years	8.8	8.8	7.7
10 Years	10.4	14.5	10.0

A Recommended Convertible Bond Fund

Fidelity Convertible Securities Fund
82 Devonshire Street
Boston, MA 02109
800-544-8888

Portfolio manager: Andrew Offit
Dividends payable: Quarterly
Sales fee: None
Annual maintenance fee: $12
  (for accounts under $2,500)
Expense ratio: 0.85%

Min. initial purchase: $2,500
  (additional: $250)
Date of inception: January 5, 1987
Net assets as of October 31, 1994:
  $958 million

Investment Objective

Fidelity Convertible Securities Fund is a no-load mutual fund that seeks a high level of total return through a combination of current income and capital appreciation by investing primarily in securities that can be converted into common stock.

Investment Policy

The fund normally invests at least 65 percent of its assets in convertible bonds and preferred stocks. the fund has the flexiblility to invest the balance in other types of securities, including corporate or U.S. debt securities, common stocks, preferred stocks, and money market instruments. The fund may invest in lower-quality, high-yielding securities although the fund expects that its fixed-income securities primarily will be rated B or better. The fund may write covered call options or buy put options.

Composition of the fund's portfolio: In late 1994 convertibles comprised 73 percent of the fund's portfolio. The fund held 25 percent of its portfolio in 33 different stocks, plus 1 percent in straight bonds and 1 percent in cash reserves.

Fund Expenses

The following table illustrates the expenses and fees you would incur as a shareholder of the fund. These expenses and fees are subject to change.

Shareholder transaction expenses

Sales load imposed on purchases:	None
Sales load imposed on reinvested dividends:	None
Deferred sales load:	None
Redemption fees:	None
Exchange fees:	None

Annual fund operating expenses

Management fee	0.52%
12b-1 fee	None
Other expenses	0.33%
Total fund operating expenses	0.85%

A feature of the Fidelity Convertible Securities Fund and other no-load funds is that shares are sold without a sales charge. Shares may be redeemed at NAV without any charge.

Performance

Fidelity's Convertible Securities Fund has been a leader among its peers during recent years. But climbing interest rates and declining stock prices in 1994 exacted a heavy toll on convertibles. The Fidelity fund, though, outperformed the group by nearly 2 percentage points, showing a loss for the year of 1.8 percent, versus a loss of 3.7 percent for its competitors. Since its inception in 1987, the fund has consistently done well, with a five-year average return of 13.7 percent, handily beating out the group's average return of 10.4 percent.

Figure 25.2 indicates total annual returns for the Fund for each full year of operation ending December 31 and comparative results of the convertible bond funds group. This is followed by total returns and the growth of $10,000 invested in the portfolio for different periods ending December 31, 1994 (assuming automatic reinvestment of income and capital gains distributions).

FIGURE 25.2 Total Return of Fidelity Convertible Securities Fund versus the Convertible Bond Funds Group

	Fund Return (%)	Group Return (%)		Fund Return (%)	Group Return (%)
1988	15.9	11.4	1992	22.0	14.3%
1989	26.3	14.4	1993	17.8	15.9
1990	-2.9	-6.0	1994	-1.8	-3.7
1991	38.7	27.8			

Periods Ending December 31, 1994	Fund Return (%)	Growth of $10,000
1 Year	-1.8	$ 9.820
3 Years	12.2	14,125
5 Years	13.7	19,002

Investment Income

Quarterly dividends from net income, when available, are paid on or about the 20th day of March, June, September, and December. Any capital gains distributions of net gain on sales of securities are paid in conjunction with the December and, if necessary, March quarterly payments.

Figure 25.3 indicates the results of a $10,000 investment made, at the beginning of 1987, assuming that capital gains distributions were reinvested in additional shares of the fund. Included in the chart are the annual income and percentage yield an investor would have received on the original investment.

The value of the original $10,000 investment was $17,234 on January 1, 1995. The fund was able to increase substantially the value of its investors' principal during the nearly eight years of operation. Income from dividends more than doubled. The performance results of Fidelity Convertible Securities Fund offer a good example of how the growth potential of an equity kicker in a portfolio, in the form of convertibles, can work to increase both an investor's principal and income.

Comments

A fairly recent entry into the convertible bond fund group, Fidelity Convertible Securities Fund has established itself as a consistently strong performer. Convertibles account for more than 70 percent of the fund's assets, and management indicates that there is no intention of

FIGURE 25.3 Annual Income and Yield on $10,000 Invested in Fidelity Convertible Securities Fund

	Shares Owned	Annual Income	Yield (%)		Shares Owned	Annual Income	Yield (%)
1987	1,000	$420	6.6	1991	1,000	$640	8.8
1988	1,000	720	6.3	1992	1,027	688	8.6
1989	1,000	770	7.3	1993	1,053	769	8.5
1990	1,000	620	7.9	1994	1,122	897	8.2

changing that allocation in the foreseeable future. In the past, though, when convertibles went as high as 85 percent of the portfolio in late 1993, the sector was reduced. Mr. Offit believed at the time that convertibles were overvalued relative to common stocks. Management remains cautious regarding convertibles, and it focuses on securities selling below par in order to minimize the fund's downside risk.

The fund's long-term performance is strong. It has soundly outperformed its peers over the last three- and five-year periods, and its sure-footedness in largely protecting principal in 1994 should reassure conservative investors.

3 Other Top Performing Convertible Bond Funds

During the five-year period ending in 1994, the following three other mutual funds categorized as convertible bond funds were leaders in their group in total return. Funds in this list are available through security brokers and carry either a front-end or back-end load.

Fund	Five-Year Average Annual Total Return (%)
MainStay Convertible Fund	14.0
Rochester Bond Fund for Growth	13.2
Pacific Horizon Capital Income Fund	12.6

Following are addresses, phone numbers, and investment performance for each fund. The charts show the year-by-year total return and dividend yield of the funds from 1990 to 1994.

MainStay Convertible Fund
260 Cherry Hill Road
Parsippany, NJ 07054
800-522-4202

Dividends payable: Quarterly
Max. sales load: 5% first year
    redemption fee
12b-1 fee: 1.00%
Expense ratio: 1.90%

Min. initial investment: $500
Date of inception: May 1, 1986
Net assets: $166 million

Investment Results 1990–1994

	Total Return (%)	Dividend Yield (%)		Total Return (%)	Dividend Yield (%)
1990	-6.7	4.3	1993	24.4	3.2
1991	48.5	2.2	1994	-1.3	4.0
1992	13.1	2.7			

Rochester Bond Fund For Growth

70 Linden Oaks
Rochester, NY 14625
716-383-1300

Dividends payable: Quarterly
Max. sales load: 3.25%
12b-1 fee: 0.75%
Expense ratio: 1.57%

Min. initial investment: $2,000
Date of inception: June 3, 1986
Net assets: $127 million

Investment Results 1990–1994

	Total Return (%)	Dividend Yield (%)		Total Return (%)	Dividend Yield (%)
1990	-8.2	5.5	1993	21.1	6.4
1991	28.6	4.8	1994	-0.8	5.4
1992	31.2	6.7			

Pacific Horizon Capital Income Fund

125 West 55th Street
New York, NY 10019
800-332-3863

Dividends payable: Quarterly
Max. sales load: 4.55
12b-1 fee: none
Expense ratio: 1.09%

Min. initial investment: $1,000
Date of inception: September 25, 1987
Net assets: $223 million

Investment Results 1990–1994

	Total Return (%)	Dividend Yield (%)		Total Return (%)	Dividend Yield (%)
1990	-6.6	5.8	1993	22.7	3.0
1991	38.2	4.5	1994	-5.9	4.2
1992	21.3	4.3			

Getting Your Bond'$ Worth!

Consider convertible bond funds if your investment objective includes capital appreciation along with current income. These funds invest in convertible securities that offer both fixed-income and capital appreciation potential. They usually have less credit risk and market risk than equity funds while providing an opportunity for you to participate in the future success of the companies into whose common shares convertibles can be exchanged. Remember, though, because potential for growth is a key feature, current yield on convertible funds generally is less than on straight bond funds.

26

☆ ☆ ☆ ☆ ☆ ☆ ☆ ☆ ☆ ☆ ☆ ☆ ☆ ☆ ☆ ☆ ☆ ☆

More Bond Funds with an Equity Kicker: 3. Flexible Funds

☆ ☆ ☆ ☆ ☆ ☆ ☆ ☆ ☆ ☆ ☆ ☆ ☆ ☆ ☆ ☆ ☆ ☆

If you are looking for a mutual fund with an equity kicker, whose management has the ability to choose freely among the different classes of assets, you may want to examine funds included in the flexible funds category.

Flexible funds typically seek to provide current income, capital appreciation, and conservation of shareholders' capital. They attempt to do this by investing in a diversified portfolio of bonds, common and preferred stocks and money market instruments. The flexibility allowed by their investment policies frequently permits these funds to invest in a variety of fixed-income instruments, including corporate bonds, mortgage-related and other asset-backed securities, convertibles, and U.S. government securities and derivatives.

Some flexible funds have produced long-term results that many investors find quite attractive. Flexible fund managers' ability to choose from the different classes of assets has paid off in times of declining bond prices. As in any mutual fund group, choosing the right fund is essential for investment success.

Over both the short and long term, the flexible funds group has produced significantly reduced returns than the S&P 500 Index. But compared with the Lehman Brothers Aggregate Bond Index, the results look better.

The average income yield for funds in this group was 3.5 percent in late 1994.

Investment Performance

Top-performing flexible funds have produced strong returns for their shareholders over the longer-term, doing much better than the group as a whole. Figure 26.1 indicates historical average annual total returns for each year from 1985 to 1994, and for different periods ending in 1994, of funds in the flexible fund group, the S&P 500 Index and the Lehman Brothers Aggregate Bond Index (LEH AGI).

FIGURE 26.1 Flexible Funds Group versus the S&P 500 Index and the Lehman Brothers Aggregate Bond Index

	S&P Group (%)	LEH 500 (%)	AGI (%)		S&P Group (%)	LEH 500 (%)	AGI (%)
1985	25.1	32.2	22.1	1990	-0.3	-3.2	8.3
1986	14.6	18.5	15.3	1991	26.9	30.6	16.0
1987	2.9	5.2	2.7	1992	8.1	7.7	7.5
1988	12.2	16.8	7.9	1993	11.9	10.1	9.8
1989	16.6	31.5	14.6	1994	-2.7	1.6	-2.1

Average Annual Total Return for Different Periods
Ending December 31, 1994

	Group (%)	S&P 500 (%)	LEH AGI (%)
1 Year	-2.7	1.6	-2.1
3 Years	5.6	6.4	4.9
5 Years	8.3	8.8	7.7
10 Years	11.1	14.5	10.0

A Recommended Flexible Fund

Berwyn Income Fund
1198 Lancaster Avenue
Berwyn, PA 19312
800-824-2249

Portfolio manager: Edward Killen   *Min. initial purchase:* $10,000
Dividends payable: Quarterly   (additional: $250)
Sales fee: None   *Date of inception:* September 3, 1987
Expense ratio: 1.00%   *Net assets as of October 31, 1994:*
                                                       $53 million

Investment Objective

The Berwyn Income Fund is a no-load mutual fund with the objective of providing investors with current income while seeking to preserve capital by taking what it considers to be reasonable risks. In pursuing its investment objective, the fund also offers the potential for capital appreciation.

Investment Policy

To achieve its objective, the fund invests in fixed-income corporate securities, preferred stocks, securities issued or guaranteed by the U.S. government, its agencies and instrumentalities, and common stocks paying cash dividends. The fixed-income corporate securities in which the fund invests include bonds, debentures, and corporate notes.

Under normal market conditions, Berwyn Income Fund will invest at least 80 percent of the value of its assets in income-producing securities. The fund may invest any percentage of its assets in investment-grade corporate debt securities, securities issued or guaranteed by the U.S. government, high yield/high risk corporate debt securities and preferred stocks. The manager determines the percentage of net assets to invest in each category of securities and the percentage of each category to hold based on prevailing economic conditions.

Investment in common stocks is limited to 25 percent of the value of the assets. But the fund may invest in fixed-income securities and preferred stocks that have common stock conversion privileges. The manager selects the fixed-income corporate debt securities primarily on the basis of current yield and secondarily on the basis of anticipated long-term return.

Composition of the Fund's Portfolio. In late 1994, bonds accounted for 27 percent of the fund's portfolio, convertibles 39 percent, preferred stocks 9 percent, common stocks 14 percent, and cash reserves 11 percent.

Fund Expenses

The following table illustrates the expenses and fees you would incur as a shareholder of the fund. These expenses and fees are subject to change.

Shareholder transaction expenses

Sales load imposed on purchases:	None
Sales load imposed on reinvested dividends:	None
Deferred sales load:	None
Redemption fees:	None
Exchange fees:	None

Annual fund operating expenses

Management fees	0.50%
12b-1 fees	None
Other expenses	0.50%
Total fund operating expenses	1.00%

A feature of the Berwyn Income Fund and other no-load funds is that shares are sold without a sales charge. Shares may be redeemed at NAV without any charge.

Performance

In its short operating history, Berwyn Income Fund has turned in a solid performance, maintaining a position in the top echelon of funds in the flexible group. The fund's concentration in high-yield corporate securities, convertible bonds and preferred stocks, and high dividend-paying common stocks, has helped its performance, particularly in recent years. During the rise in interest rates in 1994, the fund held up better than its peers in large measure due to avoiding longer-term U.S. Treasuries and utility issues.

Figure 26.2 indicates annual total returns for the Berwyn Income Fund for each full year of operation ending December 31 and comparative results of the flexible funds group. This is followed by total returns and the growth of $10,000 invested in the portfolio for different periods ending December 31, 1994 (assuming automatic reinvestment of income and capital gains distributions).

Investment Income

The Berwyn Income Fund distributes substantially all of its net investment income and any realized capital gains. Dividends from net investment income are paid quarterly. Distributions from short-term capital gains may be paid quarterly or annually; long-term capital gain distributions are paid annually.

Figure 26.3 indicates the results of a $10,000 investment made at the beginning of 1988, assuming that capital gains distributions were

FIGURE 26.2 Total Return of Berwyn Income Fund versus the Flexible Funds Group

	Fund Return (%)	Group Return (%)		Fund Return (%)	Group Return (%)
1988	12.4	12.2	1992	21.8	8.1
1989	10.8	16.6	1993	16.8	11.9
1990	-0.1	-0.3	1994	-1.1	-2.7
1991	23.0	26.9			

Periods Ending December 31, 1994	Fund Return (%)	Growth of $10,000
1 Year	-1.1	$9,890
3 Years	12.1	14,087
5 Years	11.6	17,311

FIGURE 26.3 Annual Income and Yield on $10,000 Invested in Berwyn Income Fund

	Shares Owned	Annual Income	Yield (%)		Shares Owned	Annual Income	Yield (%)
1988	1,052	$810	8.1	1992	1,072	$750	7.6
1989	1,057	835	8.4	1993	1,125	731	7.3
1990	1,063	882	8.8	1994	1,189	618	6.2
1991	1,067	992	9.9				

reinvested in additional shares of the fund. Included in the chart are the annual income and percentage yield an investor would have received on the original investment.

The value of the original $10,000 investment on January 1, 1995, was $12,810. The fund managed a modest increase in the value of its investors' principal during the seven years, but income from dividends dropped. The performance results of Berwyn Income Fund indicate the positive effect of an investment objective that includes capital appreciation. While investment income eventually declined, the total return was better than that of most bond funds that concentrated on income alone.

Comments

Berwyn Income Fund is a stable, low-risk choice for conservative income-seeking investors. It provides an above average yield and its investor-friendly no-load structure makes it all the more attractive.

The fund's management believes that its strong results in recent years have been due to three main factors:

1. its focus on the industrial sector of the corporate bond market where companies have experienced improved cash flows;
2. the fund's avoidance of risky derivative products and of leverage in the portfolio; and
3. the inclusion of inflation hedges in the stock portion of the portfolio.

The fund has managed its expenses well, having reduced them to 1.00 percent of assets in 1994 from 1.07 percent in 1993, and 1.34 percent in the prior two years. Management anticipates a further reduction in expenses as the fund continues to grow, which will help total return. Net assets of Berwyn Income Fund have grown from $4 million in 1990 to more than $52 million in late 1994.

For the future, the portfolio manager, Mr. Killen, believes that fears about inflation are excessive and that the real rate of return on long-term bonds is very attractive. He believes that long-term interest rates may have peaked and is concentrating on sectors of the economy such as basic manufacturing, capital goods (including technology issues), and natural resources. He maintains a significant commitment to forest products and steel companies.

3 Other Top Performing Flexible Funds

During the ten-year period ending in 1994, the following three other mutual funds in the flexible funds category were leaders in the group in total return. One fund in this list that is no-load or low-load and can be purchased directly is listed with an asterisk.

Fund	Ten-Year Average Annual Total Return (%)
Oppenheimer Total Return Fund	15.0
*General Securities Fund	13.1
Phoenix Income & Growth Fund	12.3

Following are addresses, phone numbers, and investment performance for each fund. The charts show the year-by-year total return and dividend yield of the funds from 1985 to 1994.

Oppenheimer Total Return Fund
3410 S. Galena Street
Denver, CO 80231
800-525-7048

Dividends payable: Quarterly   *Min. initial investment:* $1,000
Max. sales load: 5.75%   *Date of inception:* July 30, 1944
Expense ratio: 0.99%   *Net assets:* $1.3 billion

Investment Results 1985–1994

	Total Return (%)	Dividend Yield (%)		Total Return (%)	Dividend Yield (%)
1985	34.4	2.9	1990	-3.9	3.7
1986	19.7	4.4	1991	36.3	2.7
1987	12.3	4.1	1992	12.8	2.3
1988	13.3	3.9	1993	21.2	2.0
1989	19.2	3.6	1994	-7.9	2.6

*General Securities Fund
701 4th Avenue South
Minneapolis, MN 55415
800-331-4923

Dividends payable: Quarterly   *Min. initial investment:* $500
Max. sales load: None   *Date of inception:* February 27, 1951
Expense ratio: 1.50%   *Net assets:* $27 million

Investment Results 1985–1994

	Total Return (%)	Dividend Yield (%)		Total Return (%)	Dividend Yield (%))
1985	39.8	5.2	1990	-0.3	4.5
1986	9.1	2.8	1991	35.7	4.0
1987	2.2	6.3	1992	6.1	3.5
1988	14.0	5.0	1993	6.2	2.1
1989	20.4	3.0	1994	5.0	1.4

Phoenix Income & Growth Fund
1 American Row
Hartford, CT 06115
800-243-4361

Dividends payable: Quarterly   *Min. initial investment:* $500
Max. sales load: 4.75   *Date of inception:* September 7, 1940
Expense ratio: 1.23%   *Net assets:* $524 million

Investment Results 1985–1994

	Total Return (%)	Dividend Yield (%)		Total Return (%)	Dividend Yield (%))
1985	25.9	6.8	1990	-1.7	5.3
1986	21.4	5.4	1991	23.4	4.6
1987	1.5	5.6	1992	11.9	4.4
1988	17.3	6.2	1993	14.5	4.0
1989	20.5	5.4	1994	-6.3	5.3

Getting Your Bond'$ Worth!

Flexible funds can invest freely among the different classes of assets. They typically seek to provide current income and capital appreciation by investing in a diversified portfolio of bonds, stocks and money market instruments. The best flexible funds have produced strong long-term results that have increased investors' capital while paying a reasonable income. But remember, as in any mutual fund group, choosing the right fund is essential for your investment success.

27

☆ ☆ ☆ ☆ ☆ ☆ ☆ ☆ ☆ ☆ ☆ ☆ ☆ ☆ ☆ ☆ ☆

Searching for
Tax Breaks—Municipal
Bond Funds

☆ ☆ ☆ ☆ ☆ ☆ ☆ ☆ ☆ ☆ ☆ ☆ ☆ ☆ ☆ ☆ ☆

With tax-free investments one of the few remaining tax breaks available, it makes sense to look into tax-free municipal bond funds. With few exceptions, dividends received from these funds are exempt from federal income taxes. Note that, with tax-free municipal bond funds, it is the *income dividends* that are tax-free. Any capital gains you incur buying and selling mutual fund shares are not. Also, with tax-free mutual funds, capital gains earned and distributed by the fund are subject to federal, state, and local tax.

The income yield on municipal bond funds is generally lower than is available from many taxable bond funds. However, once you factor in your tax rate, a tax-free investment can often provide a higher net return. For example, suppose you are considering investing $10,000 in a municipal bond fund with a 5.5 percent yield or a taxable bond fund yielding 7.0 percent. If you're in the 36 percent tax bracket, the difference can be dramatic, as is indicated below:

	Annual Income	Taxes @ 36%	Income You Keep
Tax-free bond fund yielding 5.5%	$550	$ 0	$550
Taxable bond fund yielding 7.0%	700	252	448

With the tax-free bond fund, you keep $102 more.

It is easy to compare taxable and tax-free bond funds by looking at tax-equivalent yields. A tax-equivalent yield is what a taxable bond fund would have to pay to produce the same after-tax income as a tax-free fund. Match the tax-equivalent yield for your tax bracket to the tax-free yield in Figure 27.1 below.

National Municipal Bond Funds

National municipal bond funds invest in municipal bonds issued throughout the United States to earn income free from federal income taxes. Income may still be subject to state and local taxes. Tax-free funds are categorized by the maturity of the securities in which they invest, as follows:

Fund	Average Maturity
Tax-free money market fund	120 days or less
Short-term tax-free bond fund	1–3 years
Intermediate-term tax-free bond fund	3–10 years
Long-term tax-free bond fund	10 or more years

A municipal bond fund's yield is determined primarily by credit quality, maturity, and costs of ownership. As a general rule, you will earn a higher yield from a fund that invests in lower-quality bonds. For funds of similar credit quality, you will earn a higher yield from a

FIGURE 27.1 Equivalent Yields: Tax-Free versus Taxable Securities

Tax-Free Yields	Tax-Equivalent Yields for Different Tax Brackets				
	15%	28%	31%	36%	39.6%
3%	3.53%	4.17%	4.35%	4.69%	4.97%
4	4.71	5.56	5.80	6.25	6.62
5	5.88	6.94	7.25	7.81	8.28
6	7.06	8.33	8.70	9.38	9.93
7	8.24	9.72	10.14	10.94	11.59
8	9.41	11.11	11.59	12.50	−13.25

fund that holds bonds with longer maturities. As for costs, over time, sales charges, excessive fees, and high operating expenses have the potential to consume a large portion of your investment return.

So, in selecting a tax-free municipal bond fund, you should balance your need for income with safety and the potential for short-term principal stability. Funds holding lower-quality bonds and funds with the longest maturities, while they offer the highest yields, also expose your principal to the greatest fluctuations. And, since high costs can reduce your return, it pays to be cost-conscious.

Investment Performance

Figure 27.2 indicates historical average annual total returns for each year from 1985 to 1994, and for different periods ending in 1994, of the national municipal bond funds group and the Lehman Brothers Municipal Bond Index (LEH MUNI).

FIGURE 27.2 National Municipal Bond Funds Group versus Lehman Brothers Municipal Bond Index

	Group Return (%)	LEH MUNI Return (%)		Group Return (%)	LEH MUNI Return (%)
1985	17.9	20.1	1990	6.1	7.3
1986	16.7	19.3	1991	11.4	12.2
1987	-0.4	1.5	1992	8.3	8.8
1988	10.4	10.1	1993	11.3	12.3
1989	9.2	10.8	1994	-5.3	-5.1

**Average Annual Total Return for Different Periods
Ending December 31, 1994**

	Group Return (%)	LEH AGI Return (%)
1 Year	-5.3	-5.1
3 Years	4.5	5.1
5 Years	6.2	6.9
10 Years	8.4	9.5

A Recommended National Municipal Bond Fund

Vanguard Municipal Bond Fund Intermediate-Term Portfolio
P.O. Box 2600
Valley Forge, PA 19482
800-662-7447

Portfolio manager:	*Min. initial purchase:* $3,000
Christopher Ryon	(additional: $100)
Vanguard Group	*Date of inception:*
Dividends payable: Monthly	September 1, 1977
Sales load: None	*Net assets as of December, 1994:*
Expense ratio: 0.20%	$5 billion

Investment Objective

Vanguard Municipal Bond Fund Intermediate-Term Portfolio seeks to provide investors with the highest level of income that is exempt from federal income tax and consistent with preservation of capital.

Investment Policy

The fund invests principally in tax-exempt municipal securities. Tax-exempt municipal securities are debt obligations, issued by state and local governments and regional governmental authorities, which provide interest income that is exempt from federal income taxes. The Intermediate-Term Portfolio invests in high-quality municipal securities of varying maturities. It maintains a dollar-weighted average maturity between 7 and 12 years. There is no limit on the maturity of any individual security in the portfolio. The portfolio is intended for investors who are willing to accept moderate share price fluctuations in exchange for potentially higher and more durable yields.

At least 95 percent of the municipal securities held in the portfolio must be rated a minimum of Baa by Moody's or BBB by Standard & Poor's. No more than 20 percent of the portfolio will be held in the lowest investment grade rating. No more than 5 percent of the municipal securities may be lower-rated or unrated.

In addition, the portfolio may invest in the following short-term municipal obligations: high-quality short-term municipal notes, tax-exempt commercial paper, and municipal bonds with an effective maturity of one year or less; and unrated short-term obligations from an issuer whose outstanding long-term municipal obligations are rated a minimum of A by Moody's or Standard & Poor's.

Fund Expenses

The following table illustrates the expenses and fees you would incur as a shareholder of the fund. These expenses and fees are subject to change.

Shareholder transaction expenses

Sales load imposed on purchases:	None
Sales load imposed on reinvested dividends:	None
Redemption fees:	None
Exchange fees:	None

Annual fund operating expenses

Management fee:	0.15%
Investment advisory fees:	0.01
Other expenses:	<u>0.04</u>
Total operating expenses	0.20%

Since there is no cost to buy shares in the Vanguard Municipal Bond Fund Intermediate-Term Portfolio, all your money goes to work for you. Further, the fund's extremely low operating expenses should be a significant help to its long-term investment performance. These operating expenses are about 75 percent less than those incurred by the average fund in the national municipal bond fund group.

Performance

For the ten years ending in 1994, the Intermediate-Term Portfolio had a strong performance record (until calendar year 1994), with an average total annual return of 9.1 percent for the ten years, versus 8.4 percent for its peer group. Like most funds, the Portfolio was hurt by a -2.1 percent return in 1994, but not as badly as its peers, which had an average return of -5.3 percent.

Figure 27.3 indicates annual total returns for the Intermediate-Term Portfolio from 1985 to 1994 and comparative results of the national municipal bond funds group. This is followed by total returns and the growth of $10,000 invested in the portfolio for different periods ending in 1994 (assuming automatic reinvestment of income and capital gains distributions).

Investment Income

Dividends consisting of virtually all of the ordinary income of the Intermediate-Term Portfolio are distributed to shareholders on the first business day of each month. Capital gains distributions, if any, are paid annually.

Figure 27.4 indicates the annual income and percentage yield you would have received each year if you had made a $10,000 investment, in the beginning of January 1988, assuming that any capital gains distributions were reinvested in additional shares of the fund.

The value of the original $10,000 investment was $12,253 on January 1, 1995, an increase of $2,253 over the ten-year period. Income from dividends gradually declined, reflecting generally declining interest rates. The 40-share increase in total shares owned resulted from reinvested capital gains distributions.

FIGURE 27.3   Total Annual Returns of Vanguard Municipal Bond Fund Intermediate-Term Portfolio versus the National Municipal Bond Funds Group

	Fund Return (%)	Group Return (%)		Fund Return (%)	Group Return (%)
1985	17.3	17.9	1990	7.2	6.1
1986	16.2	16.7	1991	12.2	11.4
1987	1.6	-0.4	1992	8.9	8.3
1988	10.0	10.4	1993	11.6	11.3
1989	10.0	9.2	1994	-2.1	-5.3

	Fund Return (%)	Growth of $10,000
1 Year	-2.1	$ 9,790
3 Years	5.9	11,876
5 Years	7.4	14,290
10 Years	9.1	23,892

Comments

The Vanguard Municipal Bond Fund consists of seven portfolios, including a money market portfolio, each of which provides tax-exempt income. The portfolios have different maturity and credit quality standards. In addition, the money market portfolio seeks to a constant share price of one dollar.

Besides the Intermediate-Term Portfolio, already described, and the money market portfolio, the other portfolios are as follows:

The Short-Term Portfolio maintains an average maturity between 1 and 2 years, and purchases high-quality securities with an effective maturity of 5 years or less.

The Limited-Term Portfolio maintains an average maturity of between 2 and 5 years, and purchases high-quality securities with an effective maturity of 10 years or less.

The Long-Term Portfolio purchases high-quality securities and maintains an average maturity between 15 and 25 years. There is no limit on the maturity of any individual security in the portfolio.

The Insured Long-Term Portfolio invests at least 80 percent of its assets in insured tax-exempt municipal securities, and may invest up to 20 percent of its assets in uninsured municipals rated a minimum of A by Moody's or Standard & Poor's. The average credit rating of the securities held is expected to be the equivalent of Aaa from Moody's or AAA from Standard & Poor's. The portfolio maintains an average maturity between 15 and 25 years.

FIGURE 27.4 Annual Income and Yield on $10,000 Invested in Vanguard Municipal Bond Fund Intermediate-Term Portfolio

	Shares Owned	Annual Income	Yield (%)		Shares Owned	Annual Income	Yield (%)
1985	949	$863	8.6	1990	962	$779	7.8
1986	949	825	8.3	1991	969	755	7.6
1987	950	779	7.8	1992	975	712	7.1
1988	957	775	7.8	1993	984	689	6.9
1989	957	803	8.0	1994	989	682	6.8

The High-Yield Portfolio, in an effort to provide higher yields, invests in securities with an average credit quality lower than that of the Long-Term Portfolio. It invests at least 80 percent of its assets in investment-grade municipal securities and up to 20 percent in lower-rated or unrated municipal securities.

Several of the Vanguard Municipal Bond Fund Portfolios have produced superior performance records and are highly regarded by many investors. Their appeal is further enhanced by their very low expense structure. There are no sales charges, and operating expenses are well below those of their peers.

 3 Other Top Performing National Municipal Bond Funds

During the ten years ending in 1994, the following three mutual funds categorized as national municipal bond funds were leaders in their group in total return. The fund that has no sales load and can be purchased directly from the mutual fund company is listed with an asterisk.

Fund	Ten-Year Average Annual Total Return (%)
United Municipal Bond Fund	10.3
*Vanguard Municipal Bond Fund High-Yield Portfolio	10.0
Smith Barney Managed Municipal Bond Fund	9.9

Following are addresses, phone numbers, and investment performance for each fund. The charts show the year-by-year total return and dividend yield of the funds from 1985 to 1994.

United Municipal Bond Fund
P.O. Box 29217
Shawnee Mission, KS 66201
800-366-5465

Dividends payable: Monthly   *Min. initial investment:* $500
Max. sales load: 4.25%   *Date of inception:* September 29, 1976
Expense ratio: 0.64%   *Net assets:* $951 million

Investment Results 1985–1994

	Total Return (%)	Dividend Yield (%)		Total Return (%)	Dividend Yield (%)
1985	24.3	7.6	1990	5.6	6.6
1986	22.0	6.6	1991	13.5	5.8
1987	-1.6	7.0	1992	9.5	5.5
1988	15.0	6.5	1993	14.3	4.8
1989	11.1	6.5	1994	-7.1	5.4

*Vanguard Municipal Bond Fund High-Yield Portfolio

P.O. Box 2600
Valley Forge, PA 19482
800-662-7447

Dividends payable: Monthly   **Min. initial investment:** $3,000
Max. sales load: None   **Date of inception:** December 27, 1978
Expense ratio: 0.20%   **Net assets:** $1.7 billion

Investment Results 1985–1994

	Total Return (%)	Dividend Yield (%)		Total Return (%)	Dividend Yield (%)
1985	21.7	8.6	1990	5.9	7.3
1986	19.7	7.6	1991	14.8	6.9
1987	-1.6	7.9	1992	9.9	6.5
1988	13.8	7.4	1993	12.7	5.8
1989	11.1	7.3	1994	-5.1	6.4

Smith Barney Managed Municipal Bond Fund

388 Greenwich Street
New York, NY 10013
212-720-9218

Dividends payable: Monthly   **Min. initial investment:** $1,000
Max. sales load: 4.50%   **Date of inception:** March 4, 1981
Expense ratio: 0.72%   **Net assets:** $1.7 billion

Investment Results 1985–1994

	Total Return (%)	Dividend Yield (%)		Total Return (%)	Dividend Yield (%)
1985	20.8	7.8	1990	5.2	7.1
1986	18.7	7.0	1991	14.3	6.6
1987	0.5	7.3	1992	9.4	6.1
1988	11.6	7.1	1993	15.9	5.5
1989	10.1	6.8	1994	-4.5	6.2

Single State Municipal Bond Funds

Tax-free municipal bonds have been called the workhorse of invest-ments, and the higher your tax bracket, the harder the municipal bond pulls for you. When the additional value of exemption from state and local taxes is taken into account, the tax-free workhorse pulls even harder. Single-state municipal bond funds work just like national municipal bond funds except their portfolios contain the debt issues of just one state. A resident of that state has the advantage of receiving income that is exempt from both federal and state tax. Single-state funds are available only to investors who reside in the specified state.

Municipal bond funds are said to be triple-tax-free when they are exempt from federal, state *and* local taxes. Such funds, for example, benefit residents of New York City, who are subject to federal, New

FIGURE 27.5 Equivalent Yields: Tax-Free versus Taxable Securities

If Your Combined Federal, New York State, and New York City Tax Bracket is	To Match a Tax-Free Return of					
	3.5%	4.0%	5.0%	6.0%	7.0%	8.0%
	Your Taxable Yield Would Have to be This Much					
24.73%	4.6%	5.3%	6.6%	7.9%	9.3%	10.6%
36.25%	5.4	6.2	7.8	9.4	10.9	12.5
38.94%	5.7	6.5	8.1	9.8	11.4	13.1
43.36%	6.1	7.0	8.8	10.5	12.3	14.1
46.55%	6.5	7.4	9.3	11.2	13.1	15.0

York State and New York City income taxes. To illustrate the benefit of triple-tax-free income, Figure 27.5 below shows the taxable yields needed to match tax-free yields for residents of New York City.Concentrating your investment in one state's securities presents special risks. These risks include the possibility of a regional recession, or a change in the laws that cap a local government's ability to raise taxes to pay its debts. The municipal bonds of any one state could lose considerable value, and if you had a large part of your assets in those bonds you could be hurt.

To solve this problem, certain funds invest in *insured* bonds. Some municipalities purchase insurance for their bonds upon issuance. Such bonds are rated AAA, the highest quality rating. In the event of a default by an issuing municipality, the insured bond's remaining interest payments and principal value would be fully covered by the bond issuer's insurance company. Some mutual funds purchase insurance for high-quality bonds that have not been previously insured. This insurance has the effect of making an A-rated bond equivalent in quality to an AAA-rated bond. Remember though, the insurance feature of a municipal bond fund *does not guarantee the market value* of the municipal bonds or the value of the fund's shares. The insurance refers to the face or par value of the bonds in the fund.

Residents of California and New York have the most single-state municipal bond funds to choose from. Single state funds are now available for residents of the following states:

Alabama	Kentucky	North Carolina
Arizona	Louisiana	North Dakota
California	Maryland	Ohio
Colorado	Massachusetts	Oregon
Connecticut	Michigan	Pennsylvania
Florida	Minnesota	Rhode Island
Georgia	Missouri	Texas
Hawaii	New Jersey	Virginia
Indiana	New Mexico	Washington
Kansas	New York	

Morningstar Mutual Funds and *Value Line Mutual Fund Survey* are two services where you can find information on mutual fund companies that offer single-state municipal bond funds for your state. One or both of these services is likely to be available in your public library.

Getting Your Bond'$ Worth!

Municipal bonds offer one of the few remaining tax breaks. The tax-free income yield on municipal bond funds is generally lower than is available from many taxable bond funds, but once you factor in your tax rate, a tax-free investment can often provide a significantly higher net return. Note that, with tax-free municipal bond funds, the *income* dividends are tax-free. Any capital gains earned and distributed by the fund are subject to federal, state, and local tax.

28

☆ ☆ ☆ ☆ ☆ ☆ ☆ ☆ ☆ ☆ ☆ ☆ ☆ ☆ ☆ ☆ ☆ ☆

Bond Funds You Can
Buy at a Discount

☆ ☆ ☆ ☆ ☆ ☆ ☆ ☆ ☆ ☆ ☆ ☆ ☆ ☆ ☆ ☆ ☆ ☆

One type of bond fund is unlike open-end mutual funds in that it does not stand ready to issue and redeem shares on a continuous basis. Called "closed-end funds," these funds have a fixed capitalization represented by shares that are publicly traded, often on major stock exchanges. One interesting, and potentially profitable aspect of closed-end funds is that they are frequently available for purchase at a *discount* from their net asset value (NAV).

Like open-end bond funds, closed-end funds are operated by pooling the money of shareholders and investing that money in a diversified securities portfolio having a specified investment objective. The funds provide professional management, economies of scale, and the liquidity available with public trading on a major exchange. Even though the NAV of closed-end funds is calculated the same way as for open-end funds, the price you will pay or receive for shares traded on an exchange may be above or below the NAV. This is because the price of shares is determined on an auction market basis, the same as for all other traded shares of stock. Thus, the investor in a closed-end bond fund has an additional tier of risk, and possible profit, that the open-end fund investor does not have. The value per share responds not only to the fluctuation in value of the underlying securities in the fund's portfolio, but also to supply and demand factors that influence the fund's share price as it trades on an exchange.

Closed-end funds hold two main attractions for investors:

1. Management of a closed-end bond fund is not concerned with continuous buying and selling of securities in its portfolio to accomodate new investors and redemptions, as is the responsibility of an open-end fund and which may conflict with ideal market timing. Thus, a well-managed closed-end fund can often buy and sell on more favorable terms.

2. Shares of closed-end bond funds are frequently available for purchase at a discount from NAV.

The resulting benefit you may enjoy from these two factors is that annual earnings of closed-end funds sometimes exceeds the earnings of open-end funds with similar portfolios.

Shares of closed-end bond funds are purchased and sold through securities brokers. Commissions, which vary from broker to broker, are payable both when shares are purchased and again when they are sold. Typically, shares are traded in 100-share lots, but "odd-lots" of fewer than 100 shares may also be transacted.

The price, or *market value*, of closed-end shares is determined by supply and demand factors affecting the market. Shares may trade at a premium or at a discount relative to the NAV of the fund. Factors at work in determining share price include the composition of the portfolio, yield, the general market, and year-end tax selling. Some funds have buy-back programs designed to support the market price, reduce the number of shares outstanding and increase earnings per share.

When shares are first issued by an investment company, they tend to sell at a premium for a time and then fall back when brokers stop aggressively promoting them and turn their attention to other products. For investors, a key consideration is when to buy. The initial offering price typically reflects a 7 percent sales fee, so you can usually save money by waiting a few months to buy a new fund after the sales promotion has died down.

In addition to daily transactions of closed-end funds reported in the financial sections of major newspapers, *Barron's National Business and Financial Weekly* publishes a special section each week with a complete listing of closed-end bond funds. Closed-end funds selling at a premium or discount to NAV are also listed separately each Monday in the *New York Times* and *The Wall Street Journal.*

Like open-end bond funds, closed-end funds may be classified into different fixed-income bond groups. The five following sections present one recommended closed-end fund in each group, plus three others that have performed well in recent years. An address and phone number for each is given so you can write or call for an annual report.

 A Recommended General Corporate Bond Fund

1838 Bond Debenture Trading Fund
100 Matsonford Street
Radnor, PA 19087
610-293-4300

Portfolio manager: John Donaldson *Where traded:* NYSE
NAV (3/31/95): $20.64 *Market price (3/31/95):* $20.13
Percent difference: -2.5% *Dividends payable:* Quarterly
Management fee: 0.63% *Date of inception:* October 13, 1971

Investment Objective

1838 Bond Debenture Trading Fund seeks a high rate of return, primarily from interest income and trading activity.

Investment Policy

The fund invests at least 75 percent of its assets in higher-quality, nonconvertible debt securities. It seeks capital appreciation by engaging in short-term trading of higher-quality debt securities. The balance may be invested in other debt securities or in preferred stocks. The fund may borrow to obtain investment leverage.

Investment Income

Income distributions of the 1838 Bond Debenture Trading Fund are paid to shareholders quarterly. Net capital gains distributions, if any, have been paid in the fourth quarter. Dividend and capital gains distributions may be reinvested in additional shares or received in cash.

Figure 28.1 indicates the annual income and percentage yield you would have received each year if you had made a $10,000 investment, paying the average price of 1838 Bond Fund shares in 1985 (but not considering broker's commission), and assuming that the fund's 1992 capital gains distribution (paid in the last quarter) was invested in additional shares.

On January 1, 1995, the market value of the original $10,000 investment was $11,648. Income from dividends dropped, reflecting an environment of generally declining interest rates, but produced an average annual yield of 9.6% on the original amount invested.

3 Other Top Performing General Corporate Bond Funds

Following are three other closed-end general corporate bond funds that have performed well in recent years. The market price, NAV, and percent difference is given for each fund as of March 31, 1995. At times, funds may trade at a premium or discount to their NAVs.

CS First Boston Income Fund
12 East 49th Street
New York, NY 10017
800-541-4905

FIGURE 28.1   Annual Income and Yield on $10,000 Invested in 1838 Bond
Debenture Trading Fund

	Shares Owned	Annual Income	Yield (%)		Shares Owned	Annual Income	Yield (%)
1985	506	$1,012	10.1	1990	506	$946	9.5
1986	506	1,012	10.1	1991	506	926	9.3
1987	506	1,194	10.2	1992	506	931	9.3
1988	506	941	9.4	1993	512	896	9.0
1989	506	921	9.2	1994	512	881	8.8

Where traded: NYSE
Market price (3/31/95): $7.38
Date of inception: April 15, 1987

NAV (3/31/95): $8.22
Percent difference: -10.28%

Current Income Shares
445 South Figueroa Street
Los Angeles, CA 90017
213-236-7098

Where traded: NYSE
Market price (3/31/95): $11.25
Date of inception: March 27, 1973

NAV (3/31/95): $12.87
Percent difference: -12.59%

Transamerica Income Shares
1150 South Olive Street
Los Angeles, CA 90015
213-742-4141

Where traded: NYSE
Market price (3/31/95): $22.55
Date of inception: February 28, 1972

NAV (3/31/95): $23.37
Percent difference: -3.72%

 A Recommended High-Yield Corporate Bond Fund

USF&G Pacholder Fund
8044 Montgomery Road
Cincinnati, OH 45236
513-985-3200

Where traded: AMEX
Market price (3/31/95): $16.00
Portfolio manager: Steven Ecklund
Management fee: 0.80%

NAV (3/31/95): $16.56
Percent difference: -3.38
Dividends payable: Quarterly
Date of inception:
November 23, 1988

Investment Objective

USF&G Pacholder Fund seeks a high level of total return.

Investment Policy

The fund invests in very-high-yielding, low-rated or nonrated, fixed-income securities of U.S. companies that are generally trading at a discount to face value. Some of these companies may be experiencing financial or operating difficulties, and some companies may be involved, at the time of acquisition or soon thereafter, in reorganizations, capital restructurings, or bankruptcy proceedings.

Investment Income

Income dividends of the USF&G Pacholder Fund are paid to shareholders quarterly. Net capital gains distributions, if any, have been paid in the fourth quarter. Dividend and capital gains distributions may be reinvested in additional shares or received in cash.

Figure 28.2 indicates the annual income and percentage yield you would have received each year if you had made a $10,000 investment, paying the average price of USF&G Pacholder Fund shares in 1989 (but not considering broker's commission), and assuming that the fund's 1993 capital gains distribution (paid in the last quarter) was invested in additional shares.

On January 1, 1995, the market value of the original $10,000 investment was $12,941. Income from dividends held fairly steady during the period, producing an average annual yield of 12.2% on the original amount invested.

FIGURE 28.2 Annual Income and Yield on $10,000 Invested in USF&G Pacholder Fund

	Shares Owned	Annual Income	Yield (%)		Shares Owned	Annual Income	Yield (%)
1989	603	$1,266	12.7	1992	603	$1,260	12.6
1990	603	1,079	10.8	1993	603	1,260	12.6
1991	603	1,290	12.9	1994	609	1,146	11.5

3 Other Top Performing High-Yield Corporate Bond Funds

Following are three other closed-end high-yield corporate bond funds that have performed well in recent years. The market price, net asset value, and percent difference is given for each fund as of March 31, 1995.

High Yield Income Fund
One Seaport Plaza
New York, NY 10292
212-214-3334

Where traded: NYSE   *NAV (3/31/95):* $6.93
Market price (3/31/95): $7.63   *Percent difference:* +10.03%
Date of inception: November 6,
   1987

High Yield Plus Fund
One Seaport Plaza
New York, NY 10292
212-214-3332

Where traded: NYSE   *NAV (3/31/95):* $7.86
Market price (3/31/95): $8.00   *Percent difference:* +1.78%
Date of inception: April 22, 1988

CIGNA High Income Shares
1350 Main Street
Springfield, MA 01103
800-523-3700

Where traded: NYSE   *NAV (3/31/95):* $6.84
Market price (3/31/95): $7.25   *Percent difference:* +5.99%
Date of inception: August 10,
   1988

A Recommended Government Bond Fund

Mentor Income Fund
901 East Byrd Street
Richmond, VA 23219
800-472-0090

Where traded: NYSE   *NAV (3/31/95):* $9.70
Market price (3/31/95): $8.83   *Percent difference:* -8.51%
Portfolio manager: W. West, Jr. *Dividends payable:* Monthly
   and M. Jones   *Date of inception:* December 30, 1988
Management fee: 0.65%

Investment Objective

Mentor Income Fund seeks high income consistent with preservation of capital.

Investment Policy

The fund invests primarily in Government National Mortgage Association (GNMA) and Federal National Mortgage Association (FNMA) mortgage-backed securities. It may also invest in other mortgage-related securities, such as collateral mortgage obligations, and in asset-backed securities. The fund invests at least 80 percent of its assets in the two highest investment grade categories. No more than 20 percent of its assets may be held in issues rated A.

Investment Income

Income dividends of the Mentor Income Fund are paid to shareholders monthly. No capital gains distributions were paid through 1994. Income dividends and capital gains distributions, if any, may be reinvested in additional shares or received in cash.

Figure 28.3 indicates the annual income and percentage yield you would have received each year if you had made a $10,000 investment, paying the average price of Mentor Income Fund shares in 1989 (but not considering broker's commission).

FIGURE 28.3 Annual Income and Yield on $10,000 Invested in Mentor
Income Fund

	Shares Owned	Annual Income	Yield (%)		Shares Owned	Annual Income	Yield (%)
1989	914	$ 959	9.6	1992	914	$1,124	11.2
1990	914	1,169	11.7	1993	914	941	9.4
1991	914	1,151	11.5	1994	914	877	8.8

On January 1, 1995, the market value of the original $10,000 investment was $9,254. Income from dividends gradually declined during the period, producing an average annual yield of 10.4% on the original amount invested.

3 Other Top Performing Government Bond Funds

Following are three other closed-end government bond funds that have performed well in recent years. The market price, NAV, and percent difference is given for each fund as of March 31, 1995.

Blackrock Target Term Trust
One Seaport Plaza
New York, NY 10292
800-451-3332

Where traded: NYSE
Market price (3/31/95): $8.75
Date of inception: November 8, 1988

NAV (3/31/95): $9.44
Percent difference: -7.31%

Blackrock Income Trust
One Seaport Plaza
New York, NY 10292
800-451-6788

Where traded: NYSE
Market price (3/31/95): $7.00
Date of inception: July 22, 1988

NAV (3/31/95): $7.45
Percent difference: -6.04%

Dean Witter Government Income Trust
Two World Trade Center
New York, NY 10048
800-869-3863

Where traded: NYSE
Market price (3/31/95): $7.83
Date of inception: February 29, 1988

NAV (3/31/95): $8.84
Percent difference: -10.92%

 A Recommended International Bond Fund

Global Income Plus Fund
1285 Avenue of the Americas
New York, NY 10019
800-647-1568

Where traded: NYSE
Market price (3/31/95): $8.38
Portfolio manager: N. Fachler and
   S. Waugh
Date of inception: September 1, 1988

NAV (3/31/95): $8.91
Percent difference: -6.0%
Dividends payable: Quarterly
Management fee: 0.85%

Investment Objective

Global Income Plus Fund seeks high current income. Capital appreciation is secondary.

Investment Policy

The fund invests at least 65 percent of its assets in debt securities rated AA and above that are denominated in foreign currencies or in U.S. mortgage-backed securities. It may invest up to 35 percent in issues rated below AA.

Investment Income

Income dividends of Global Income Plus Fund are paid to shareholders quarterly. Capital gains distributions have been paid in the last quarter. Income dividends and capital gains distributions (if any) may be reinvested in additional shares or received in cash.

Figure 28.4 indicates the annual income and percentage yield you would have received each year if you had made a $10,000 investment, paying the average price of Global Income Plus Fund shares in 1989 (but not considering broker's commission).

On January 1, 1995, the market value of the original $10,000 investment was $10,539. Income from dividends fluctuated during the period, producing an average annual yield of 10.2% on the original amount invested.

3 Other Top Performing International Bond Funds

Following are three other closed-end international bond funds that have performed well in recent years. The market price, NAV, and percent difference is given for each fund as of March 31, 1995.

First Australia Prime Income Fund
One Seaport Plaza
New York, NY 10292
800-451-6788

Where traded: AMEX   *NAV (3/31/95):* $8.71
Market price (3/31/95): $8.00   *Percent difference:* -8.15%
Date of inception: April 24, 1986

FIGURE 28.4   Annual Income and Yield on $10,000 Invested in Global
Income Plus Fund

	Shares Owned	Annual Income	Yield (%)		Shares Owned	Annual Income	Yield (%)
1989	1,102	$ 705	7.1	1992	1,131	$ 927	9.3
1990	1,131	1,334	13.3	1993	1,137	921	9.2
1991	1,131	1,097	11.0	1994	1,155	1,108	11.1

Templeton Global Income Fund
700 Central Avenue
St. Petersburg, FL 33701
800-237-0738

Where traded: NYSE
Market price (3/31/95): $6.63
Date of inception: March 24, 1988

NAV (3/31/95): $7.67
Percent difference: -13.62%

Global Government Plus Fund
One Seaport Plaza
New York, NY 10292
800-451-6788

Where traded: NYSE
Market price (3/31/95): $6.00
Date of inception: July 31, 1987

NAV (3/31/95): $7.35
Percent difference: -18.37%

A Recommended Municipal Bond Fund (National)

Putnam Managed Municipal Income Trust
One Post Office Square
Boston, MA 02109
800-634-1587

Where traded: NYSE
Market price (3/31/95): $10.13
Portfolio manager: William H. Reeves
Management fee: 0.70%

NAV (3/31/95): $9.86
Percent difference: +2.06%
Dividends payable: Monthly
Date of inception:
February 16, 1989

Investment Objective

Putnam Managed Municipal Income Trust seeks to provide a high level of current income exempt from federal income tax.

Investment Policy

The fund invests in a diversified portfolio of tax-exempt municipal securities that, in the opinion of the manager, do not threaten income or principal. It may invest up to 50 percent of its assets in municipal securities rated BB or lower, although not lower than a B-rating. The fund may use options and futures for hedging purposes.

Investment Income

Income dividends of the fund are paid to shareholders monthly. Capital gains distributions have been paid in the last quarter. Income dividends and capital gains distributions, if any may be reinvested in additional shares or received in cash.

Figure 28.5 indicates the annual income and percentage yield you would have received each year if you had made a $10,000 investment, paying the average price of Putnam Managed Municipal Income Trust shares in 1989 (but not considering broker's commission).

On January 1, 1995, the market value of the original $10,000 investment was $11,514. Income from dividends fluctuated during the period, producing an average annual yield of 7.6% on the original amount invested.

FIGURE 28.5   Annual Income and Yield on $10,000 Invested in Putnam Managed Municipal Income Trust

	Shares Owned	Annual Income	Yield (%)		Shares Owned	Annual Income	Yield (%)
1989	1,019	$632*	7.2*	1992	1,019	$774	7.7
1990	1,019	774	7.7	1993	1,027	780	7.8
1991	1,019	774	7.7	1994	1,035	786	7.9

*Annualized. Fund began operating on February 16.

3 Other Top Performing Municipal Bond Funds

Following are three other closed-end municipal bond funds (national) that have performed well in recent years. The market price, NAV, and percent difference is given for each fund as of March 31, 1995.

Kemper Strategic Municipal Income Trust
120 South LaSalle Street
Chicago, IL 60603
800-537-6006

Where traded: NYSE   *NAV (3/31/95):* $11.94
Market price (3/31/95): $11.63   *Percent difference:* -2.64%
Date of inception: March 22, 1989

MFS Municipal Income Trust
500 Boylston Street
Boston, MA 02116
800-225-2606

Where traded: NYSE   *NAV (3/31/95):* $8.87
Market price (3/31/95): $9.25   *Percent difference:* +4.28%
Date of inception: November 25,
   1986

Municipal High Income Fund
Two World Trade Center
New York, NY 10048
212-298-7350

Where traded: NYSE   *NAV (3/31/95):* $9.25
Market price (3/31/95): $8.83   *Percent difference:* -4.05%
Date of inception: November 28,
   1988

Getting Your Bond's Worth!

You can sometimes buy shares of bond funds at a discount from net asset value. This is possible with closed-end funds, which are unlike open-end mutual funds in that they are publicly traded, often on major stock exchanges. Because shares of a closed-end fund are publicly traded, you have potential for profit (or loss) from both changes in the fund's NAV *and* from changes in its market value.

Appendix

☆ ☆ ☆ ☆ ☆ ☆ ☆ ☆ ☆ ☆ ☆ ☆ ☆ ☆ ☆ ☆ ☆ ☆

Sources of Investment Analysis and Information

☆ ☆ ☆ ☆ ☆ ☆ ☆ ☆ ☆ ☆ ☆ ☆ ☆ ☆ ☆ ☆ ☆ ☆

Whether you plan to make just a single bond or bond fund investment, or to maintain an ongoing investment program, it is important to have complete and accurate information. Only then is sound judgment even possible.

The list of sources in this appendix will help you avoid the time-consuming process of finding the information that you will most likely need in managing your bond or bond fund investments. Though it is not exhaustive, the sources listed are those most commonly used by individual investors. The goal is to give you an overview of what each source supplies, together with phone numbers and addresses so that you can contact them directly.

Most public libraries subscribe to one or more investment research services. The larger ones have several. Each service takes its own approach, but they all strive for accuracy and completeness. Usually they are written in a style that is easy for the nonprofessional, part-time investor to understand. Look them over, and use the ones that suit you best. A little study will give you the confidence you need to trust in your own judgment.

You may want the convenience of a personal copy of one or more services. Some are inexpensive; others can be quite pricey. So, you will probably want to make use of your public library, at least initially.

American Association of Individual Investors (AAII)
625 North Michigan Avenue
Chicago, IL 60611-3110
312-280-0170

AAII is a non-profit corporation recognized under Section 501(C)(3) of the Internal Revenue Code as a public educational organization. Membership in the organization entitles you to several important benefits. All members receive the *AAII Journal,* the *AAII Year-End Tax Guide, AAII Quoteline,* a listing of companies with dividend reinvestment plans (DRIPs) and an annual stock brokerage survey. Other services include investment seminars, home study programs, a computer users' newsletter and local chapter membership.

Barron's
Dow Jones & Company
200 Burnett Road
Chicopee, MA 01020
800-628-9320

This national business and financial weekly is available by subscription and at newsstands. Barron's contains articles discussing investment trends and the Market Laboratory section provides a large amount of useful statistical data. The newspaper also contains data on individual stocks, bonds, mutual funds and government securities.

Dearborn Financial Publishing, Inc.
155 North Wacker Drive
Chicago, IL 60606-1719
800-829-7934

The Mutual Fund Encyclopedia, an annual by Gerald W. Perritt, profiles more than 3,400 no-load, low-load and load funds. Each profile gives a detailed statement of objectives and strategies and provides key financial statistics, including assets under management, current yield, portfolio turnover ratio, risk factors, and year-by-year and five-year total returns. The minimum initial investment for each fund is noted, as well as the cost of investing in each fund and the company address and toll-free number.

Investment Company Institute
1401 H Street NW
Suite 1200
Washington, DC 20005
202-326-5800

The Investment Company Institute is the national association of the American mutual fund industry. It produces a number of publications than an investor will find helpful. The *Mutual Fund Fact Book,* a basic guide to the mutual fund industry, provides annually updated facts and figures on the U.S. mutual fund industry, including trends in sales, assets, and performance. The *Directory of Mutual Funds* is published annually by the Institute. In addition to mutual fund names addresses and telephone numbers (many are toll-free), the directory lists each fund's assets, initial and subsequent investment requirements, fees charged, where to buy shares and other pertinent details. An extensive introductory text serves as a short course in mutual fund investing.

Moody's Investors Service
99 Church Street
New York, NY 10007
212-553-0547

The monthly *Bond Record* provides summary statistical information on corporate bonds and the Moody ratings for municipal bonds. Statistics on corporate bonds include quality ratings, yield-to-maturity, recent and historical price ranges, and current yield.

Morningstar, Inc.
225 West Wacker Drive
Chicago, IL 60606
800-876-5005

Morningstar offers a variety of thoroughly documented services. *Morningstar Mutual Funds* ranks among the most comprehensive, timely and useful sources for mutual fund information. Vital information for tracking, analyzing, comparing, and choosing mutual funds is condensed on a single page for each of the more than 1,200 mutual funds and is presented in one hardcover binder. Every two weeks Morningstar provides subscribers with a 32-page report summarizing the current performance of more than 1,200 funds. The bi-weekly *Morningstar Closed-End Funds,* provides complete profiles on 284 of the most actively traded closed-end funds, including many bond funds. Three-month trial subscriptions are available.

Standard & Poor's Corporation
25 Broadway
New York NY 10004
800-221-7940

Standard & Poor's Corporation's highly respected publications cover virtually the full spectrum of investor needs. Some of the most widely used include the *Bond Guide, Corporation Records, Mutual Fund Profiles,* and *Register of Corporations.* The monthly *Bond Guide* provides summary statistical information on corporate and foreign bonds, including quality ratings redemption provisions, recent price ranges, current yield, and yield-to-maturity. The guide also provides the S&P ratings for larger municipal bond issues.

Value Line Publishing, Inc.
220 East 42nd Street
New York, NY 10017-5891
800-284-7607

Value Line Convertibles surveys more than 90 percent of U.S. convertible bonds and preferred stocks. The service provides a list of recommended securities, as well as news and an evaluation of each issue. A two-month trial subscription is available. *Value Line Mutual Fund Survey* offers full-page analyses of 1,500 funds encompassing a wide range of investment objectives, which include performance data, portfolio data, tax data and so on. A three-month trial is available.

Getting Your Bond'$ Worth!

Successful investing depends on being informed. Many of the best sources of information are advertised regularly in *The Wall Street Journal, Barron's,* and *Investor's Business Daily.* Check your public library for some of the most useful investment publications. Choose the ones that suit you best. A little study will give you the confidence you need to trust in your own judgment.

Glossary

☆ ☆ ☆ ☆ ☆ ☆ ☆ ☆ ☆ ☆ ☆ ☆ ☆ ☆ ☆ ☆ ☆ ☆

adjustable-rate mortgages (ARMs): mortgage loans on which the interest rate charged by the lender is adjusted in accordance with a stipulated cost of funds index, such as the yield on one-year U.S. Treasury bills.

American Stock Exchange (AMEX): the stock exchange located at 86 Trinity Place in New York City. Stocks and bonds traded on the AMEX are generally those of small to medium-size companies.

basis point: the smallest measure used in quoting yields on bonds and notes. One basis point is 0.01 percent of yield. Thus, a bond's yield that changes from 7.54 percent to 8.44 percent is said to have gone up 90 basis points.

bear market: a prolonged period of falling prices.

bill (Treasury or t-bill): a government security with a maturity of a year or less.

bond: an interest-bearing or discounted government or corporate security that obligates the issuer to pay the bondholder a specified sum of money, usually at specific intervals, and to repay the principal amount of the loan at maturity.

bond funds: regulated investment companies whose assets are invested in diversified portfolios of bonds.

bond rating: a method of evaluating the possibility of default by a bond issuer.

bull market: a prolonged rise in the prices of stocks, bonds, or commodities. A bull market is characterized by high trading volume and usually lasts at least a few months.

callable bond: a bond which the issuer is permitted or required to redeem before the stated maturity date at a specified price, usually at or above par, by giving notice of redemption in a manner specified in the bond contract.

call protection: the length of time during which a security cannot be redeemed by the issuer.

capital gain: the difference between an asset's purchase price and selling price, when the difference is positive.

capital loss: the difference between an asset's purchase price and selling price, when the difference is negative.

cash equivalents: instruments or investments of such high liquidity and safety that they are virtually as good as cash. Examples include money market funds and Treasury bills.

closed-end fund: a type of fund that has a fixed number of shares. Unlike open-end mutual funds, it does not stand ready to issue and redeem shares on a continuous basis. Closed-end funds are generally listed on major stock exchanges.

collateral trust bond: a corporate debt security backed by other securities, usually held by a bank or other trustee.

commercial paper: short-term obligations with maturities ranging from 2 to 270 days issued by banks, corporations, and other borrowers.

common stock: units of ownership of a public corporation, usually with the right to vote and to receive dividends.

constant dollar investment plan: a system of accumulating assets by investing a fixed amount of dollars in securities at set intervals. Also called dollar cost averaging.

conversion premium: the amount by which the price of a convertible security exceeds the market price of the underlying stock.

conversion price: the dollar value at which convertible bonds, debentures or preferred stock can be converted into common stock.

conversion ratio: the relationship that determines how many shares of common stock will be received in exchange for each convertible bond or preferred share when the conversion takes place.

convertibles: preferred stock or bonds that are exchangeable for a set number of another form of securities (usually common stock) at a prestated price.

corporate bond: a debt instrument issued by a private corporation, as distinct from a governmental agency or municipality.

cost basis: the original price of an asset, used in determining capital gains.

coupon: the interest rate on a debt security the issuer promises to pay to the holder until maturity, expressed as an annual percentage of face value.

credit rating: a formal evaluation of a company's credit history and capability of repaying obligations.

credit risk: the possibility that a bond issuer will fail to make timely payments of principal and interest to a bondholder.

current maturity: the interval between the present time and the maturity date of a bond issue.

current yield: the annual interest on a bond divided by the market price, stated as a percentage.

debenture: a general debt obligation backed only by the integrity of the borrower and documented by an agreement called an indenture.

debt instrument: a written promise to repay a debt such as a bill, note, bond, banker's acceptance, certificate of deposit, or commercial paper.

deep discount bond: a bond selling for a discount of more than about 20 percent from its face value.

default: the failure of a debtor to make timely payments of interest and principal as they come due or to meet some other provision of a bond indenture.

derivative: a financial instrument that derives its market value from some specified benchmark such as a currency, commodity, interest rate, or any number of combined benchmarks.

discount: the difference between a bond's current market price and its face or redemption value.

discount broker: a brokerage firm that executes orders to buy and sell securities at commission rates lower than those charged by full service brokers.

diversification: spreading risk by placing assets in several categories of investments, such as stocks, bonds, mutual funds, etc.

dollar cost averaging: a method of accumulating assets by investing a fixed amount of dollars in securities at set intervals.

duration: A bond's duration indicates the time it will take an investor to recoup his investment. Unlike average maturity, duration reflects both principal and interest payments. Generally, the higher the coupon rate on a bond, the lower its duration will be.

equivalent taxable yield: comparison of the taxable yield on a corporate bond and the tax-free yield on a municipal bond.

Eurobond: a bond denominated in U.S. dollars or other currencies and sold to investors outside the country whose currency is used.

expense ratio: the proportion that annual expenses, including all costs of operation, bear to average net assets for the year.

face value: the value of a bond, note, mortgage, or other security as given on the certificate or instrument.

Fannie Mae: nickname for the Federal National Mortgage Association.

Federal Home Loan Mortgage Corporation (FHLMC or "Freddie Mac"):   a federally created corporation established to facilitate the financing of single-family residential housing by creating and maintaining an active secondary market for conventional home mortgages.

Federal National Mortgage Association (FNMA or "Fannie Mae"):   a publicly owned, government-sponsored corporation chartered in 1938 to purchase mortgages from lenders and resell them to investors.

first call date: the first date specified in the indenture of a corporate or municipal bond contract on which part or all of the bond may be redeemed at a set price.

Fitch Investors Service, Inc.:   a New York and Denver-based rating firm, which rates corporate and municipal bonds, preferred stock, commercial paper, and other obligations.

fixed-income investment: a security that pays a fixed rate of return.

floating rate note: a debt instrument with a variable interest rate.

Freddie Mac: nickname for the Federal Home Loan Mortgage Corporation.

general obligation (GO) bond: a municipal bond backed by the full faith and credit (taxing and borrowing power) of a municipality.

Government National Mortgage Association (GNMA or "Ginnie Mae"): an agency of the federal Department of Housing and Urban Development empowered to provide special assistance in financing home mortgages which is responsible for management and liquidation of federally owned mortgage portfolios.

high-grade bond: a bond rated triple-A or double-A by Standard & Poor's or Moody's rating services.

income bond: an obligation on which the payment of interest is contingent on sufficient earnings from year to year.

interest: the amount paid by a borrower as compensation for the use of borrowed money. This amount is generally expressed as an annual percentage of the principal amount.

index: a statistical composite that measures changes in the economy or in financial markets, often expressed in percentage changes from one period to another.

index fund: a mutual fund whose portfolio matches that of a broad-based index and whose performance mirrors the market as a whole.

indexing: weighting one's portfolio to match a broad-based index such as Standard & Poor's 500 so as to match its performance.

indicated yield: the coupon or dividend rate as a percentage of the current market price.

interest rate risk: the potential for fluctuations in the principal value of a bond investment caused by changes in market interest rates.

inverted yield curve: an unusual situation where short-term interest rates are higher than long-term rates.

investment company: a firm that invests the pooled funds of small investors in securities appropriate for its stated investment objectives.

investment grade: the broad credit designation given bonds which have a high probability of being paid and minor, if any, speculative features. Bonds rated Baa and higher by Moody's Investors Service, In.c or BBB and higher by Standard & Poor's Corporation are deemed by those agencies to be investment grade.

junk bond: a bond rated lower than Baa/BBB, also called a high-yield bond. Junk bonds are speculative compared with investment grade bonds.

Lehman Brothers Aggregate Bond Index: an index of more than 6000 fixed-income securities, encompassing U.S. Treasury and government agency securities, mortgage-backed obligations, and investment-grade corporate bonds.

liquidity: a measure of a firm's ability to meet maturing short-term obligations.

listed security: a stock or bond that has been accepted for trading by one of the organized and registered securities exchanges in the United States.

long bond: 30-year U.S. Treasury bonds, or any bond that matures in more than ten years.

marketable securities: securities that may be easily sold.

market price: the last reported price at which a security was sold on an exchange, or the combined bid and asked prices for securities traded over-the-counter.

market value: the current market price of a security.

market value-weighted index: an index whose components are weighted according to the total market value of their outstanding shares.

maturity or maturity date: the date on which the principal amount of a debt instrument becomes due and payable.

medium-term bond: a bond with a maturity of 2 to 10 years.

money market: the market for short-term debt instruments such as commercial paper, negotiable certificates of deposits, banker's acceptances, Treasury bills and discount notes of federal agencies.

money market fund: an open-ended mutual fund that invests in short-term debt instruments and pays money market rates of interest.

mortgage: a debt instrument by which the borrower (mortgagor) gives the lender (mortgagee) a lien on property as security for the repayment of a loan.

municipal bond: a debt obligation of a state or local government entity, as a city, town, village, county or special district. A prime feature of such a security is that interest on them is generally exempt from federal income taxes and, in some cases, state and local taxes too.

mutual fund: a fund operated by an investment company that raises money from shareholders and invests it in stocks, bonds, options, commodities or money market securities.

Nasdaq: the automated quotation system owned and operated by the National Association of Securities Dealers.

negative yield curve: a situation in which yields on short-term securities are higher than those on long-term securities of the same quality.

net asset value (NAV):   a mutual fund's share price on a given day, NAV is calculated by dividing the value of fund net assets by the number of shares outstanding.

net yield: the rate of return on a security net of out-of-pocket costs connected with its purchase, such as commissions or markups.

New York Stock Exchange (NYSE):   the oldest (1972) and largest stock exchange in the United States, located at 11 Wall Street in New York City.

no-load fund: a mutual fund offered by an open-end investment company that imposes no sales charge (load) on its shareholders.

noncallable: preferred stock or a bond that cannot be redeemed at the option of the issuer.

note: a debt obligation similar to a bond, but with a maturity date less than five years from the date of issue.

odd lot: a securities trade made for less than the normal trading unit, or round lot. For stocks, any purchase or sale of less than 100 shares.

over-the-counter (OTC):   a market in which securities transactions are conducted through a telephone and computer network connecting dealers in stocks and bonds, rather than on the floor of an exchange.

paper: any short-term debt security.

paper profit or loss: unrealized capital gain or loss in an investment or portfolio. Such a gain or loss becomes realized only when the security is sold.

par: the nominal or face value of a security. The par value is the amount on which interest payments are calculated.

passive investing: investing by a mutual fund that replicates a market index, such as the S&P 500 Index, thus assuring investment performance equivalent to the market as a whole.

pass-through security: a security, representing pooled debt obligations repackaged as shares, that passes income from debtors through the intermediary to investors.

payment date: the date on which a declared stock dividend or a bond interest payment is scheduled to be paid.

portfolio: a combined holding of more than one stock, bond, commodity, cash equivalent, or other asset by an individual or institutional investor.

portfolio turnover ratio: the extent to which a mutual fund's portfolio is turned over during the course of a year. It is calculated by dividing the lesser of a fund's purchases or sales (expressed in dollars and excluding all securities with maturities of less than one year) by the fund's average monthly assets.

positive yield curve: a situation in which interest rates are higher on long-term debt securities than on short-term debt securities of the same quality.

preferred stock: a normally non-voting class of capital stock that pays dividends at a specified rate and that has preference over common stock in the payment of dividends and the liquidation of assets.

premium: the amount by which a bond sells above its par (face) value.

price-earnings (PE) ratio: the price of a stock divided by its earnings per share over a 12-month period.

price-weighted index: an index in which component stocks are weighted by their price, giving higher priced stocks greater impact on the index than those at lower prices.

principal amount: the face value of a bond that must be repaid at maturity, as distinguished from the interest.

prospectus: a formal written offer to sell securities that sets forth the plan for a proposed business enterprise or mutual fund, or the facts about an existing one that an investor needs to make an informed decision.

public offering: an offering to the investment public of new securities at a price agreed upon between the issuers and the investment bankers.

ratings: designations used by investors' services to give relative indications of credit quality.

realized profit (or loss):   the profit or loss resulting from the sale or other disposal of a security.

redemption: repayment of a debt security or preferred stock issue, at or before maturity, at par or at a premium price.

registered representative: an employee of a stock exchange member broker/dealer who acts as an account executive for customers.

repurchase agreement: the purchase of a security at one price and simultaneous agreement to sell it back at a higher price.

return: profit on a securities investment, usually expressed as an annual percentage rate.

revenue bond: a municipal bond payable solely from net or gross non-tax revenues derived from tolls, charges or rents paid by users of the facility constructed with the proceeds of the bond issue.

Securities and Exchange Commission (SEC):   a federal agency created by the Securities Exchange Act of 1934 to administer that act and the Securities Act of 1933. The SEC works to promote full disclosure of publicly traded securities and to protect investors against malpractice in the securities markets.

security: an instrument evidencing debt of or equity in an enterprise in which a person invests on the expectation of financial gain. The term includes notes, stocks, bonds, debentures, or other forms of negotiable and non-negotiable evidences of indebtedness or ownership.

secured bond: a bond backed by the pledge of collateral, a mortgage, or other lien.

share: unit of equity ownership in a corporation.

stock: the ownership of a corporation represented by shares that are a claim on the corporation's earnings and assets.

stock exchange: an organized marketplace in which stocks and bonds are traded by members of the exchange, acting both as agents and principals.

STRIPS: the U.S. Treasury's acronym for Separate Trading of Registered Interest and Principal of Securities, its own zero-coupon securities. These are U.S. Treasury bonds that have been separated into their principal and coupon components, which are then sold separately as zero-coupon securities.

strips: U.S. Treasury or municipal securities that brokerage firms have separated into principal and interest which, represented by certificates, are marketed as zero-coupon securities.

taxable-equivalent yield: the interest rate which must be received on a taxable security to provide the holder the same after-tax return as that earned on a tax-exempt security.

tax basis: the price at which a security was purchased, plus brokerage commissions.

tax-exempt money market fund: a money market fund invested in short-term municipal securities and distributes tax-free income to shareholders.

tax-exempt security: an obligation, often called a municipal bond, whose interest is exempt from federal, state, and/or local taxation.

term: the time during which interest payments will be made on a bond or certificate of deposit.

total return: the percentage increase or decrease in the value of an investment over a stated period of time. A total return percentage includes both changes in value of an investment and income.

Treasury Direct: a system through which an investor can invest in U.S. Treasury securities through Federal Reserve Banks, bypassing banks or broker/dealers and avoiding their fees.

triple-tax-exempt: municipal bonds in which interest is exempt from federal, state, and local taxation for residents of the states and municipalities that issue them.

underwriter: an investment banker who agrees to purchase a new issue of securities from an issuer and distribute it to investors.

unlisted security: a security that is not listed on an organized exchange and is traded in the over the counter market.

unrealized profit (or loss): a profit or loss that has not become actual because the security has not been sold.

unsecured debt: an obligation not backed by the pledge of specific collateral.

volatile: used to describe a security characterized by rapid and extreme fluctuations in price.

warrant: a security, typically issued with preferred stock or bonds, that gives the holder the right to buy a proportionate amount of common stock at a specified price, usually at a price that is higher than the market price at the time of issuance of the warrant. The right may last for a period or indefinitely.

yankee bonds: dollar-denominated bonds issued in the U.S. by foreign banks and corporations.

yield: the percentage rate of return paid on a security, calculated by dividing its annual dividend or interest income by its cost to the investor.

zero-coupon security: a security that makes no periodic interest payments but instead is sold at a deep discount from its face value.

Index

☆ ☆ ☆ ☆ ☆ ☆ ☆ ☆ ☆ ☆ ☆ ☆ ☆ ☆ ☆ ☆ ☆ ☆